SCAPEGOAT
THE TOMMY LEE HINES STORY

PEGGY ALLEN TOWNS

authorHOUSE

AuthorHouse™
1663 Liberty Drive
Bloomington, IN 47403
www.authorhouse.com
Phone: 833-262-8899

© 2020 Peggy Allen Towns. All rights reserved.

No part of this book may be reproduced, stored in a retrieval system, or transmitted by any means without the written permission of the author.

Published by AuthorHouse 11/05/2020

ISBN: 978-1-6655-0428-7 (sc)
ISBN: 978-1-6655-0427-0 (hc)
ISBN: 978-1-6655-0470-6 (e)

Library of Congress Control Number: 2020920441

Print information available on the last page.

Any people depicted in stock imagery provided by Getty Images are models, and such images are being used for illustrative purposes only.
Certain stock imagery © Getty Images.

This book is printed on acid-free paper.

Because of the dynamic nature of the Internet, any web addresses or links contained in this book may have changed since publication and may no longer be valid. The views expressed in this work are solely those of the author and do not necessarily reflect the views of the publisher, and the publisher hereby disclaims any responsibility for them.

On occasion offensive racial labels are used in this book. Such words reflect the attitudes and principles of our society during that time and are important if we are to expose our history in its true content. I regret any insult it may cause.

The last names of sexual assault victims have not been used for the protection of their privacy. The information however is of public record and included in some newspaper clippings.

Contents

Acknowledgements xi
Prologue xiii
Chapter 1   A Disturbance 1
Chapter 2   Profiled 4
Chapter 3   Horror 6
Chapter 4   The Rally 11
Chapter 5   Blame 17
Chapter 6   God's In-Crowd 29
Chapter 7   The Move 31
Chapter 8   Nose to Nose 41
Chapter 9   The Trial 48
Chapter 10 "It Doesn't Fit" 60
Chapter 11 Verdict 66
Chapter 12 What Lies Ahead 84
Chapter 13 Looming Danger 91
Chapter 14 Not an Ordinary Parade 98
Chapter 15 What Do You See 106
Epilogue 117
Bibliography 119
Index 127
About the Author 133

Dedicated to
Tommy Lee Hines
October 10, 1952 - February 1, 2020
And
the many foot soldiers who marched and prayed
against injustice.

All events described in this book are true, and the author witnessed many of them firsthand.

Discover

"…to obtain knowledge of; arrive at through research
or study; to learn or reveal; to expose."

Webster Dictionary

Scapegoat

"A person or group made to bear the blame
for others or to suffer in their place."
"Chiefly **Biblical**. A goat let loose in the wilderness on
Yom Kippur after the high priest symbolically laid the sins
of the people on its head. Leviticus 16:8, 10, 26."

Dictionary.com

"Not everything that is faced can be changed,
but nothing can be changed until it is faced."

James Baldwin

Acknowledgements

First and foremost, I praise God for giving me the courage to revisit this story. The three year journey of research and finally writing has brought back so many memories that had been filed away in the recesses of time.

I am indebted to many, first my parents, George and Myrtle Allen, who gave me a foundation to build on, in telling our stories. I appreciate the constant reminder, "If you don't know where you've been, you'll never know where you are going."

Many thanks to those who did not put me off and agreed to share their memories of this historic civil rights movement in Decatur. You know who you are.

To those of you who believed the Tommy Lee Hines story should be told and convinced me to write this book, I am grateful. I appreciate your support during this undertaking, even if it was the simple words, "Get back on Tommy Lee," or "How is the book coming along?" To my writer's group – John Bush, Judy Rich and Joyce Pettis – you inspire me so. Thank you for taking this journey with me.

I owe a tremendous debt of thanks to the Alabama Department of Archives and History and the Morgan County Archives. The photographs and documents capture the moment and significantly contribute to telling this narrative. I am thankful for information obtained from the Rose Library, Emory University, Atlanta, Georgia, and the University of Massachusetts, Amherst, Massachusetts. I also appreciate those reporters who dared to write numerous newspaper and various other articles reporting the truth during the course of this tumultuous time.

I am extremely grateful to my circle of family and friends, who took the time to peruse a chapter for me and before you got back to me, I had changed it: Cynthia Allen, Emma Allen, and Latrisha Peterson.

Finally, in these unsettling times, when systemic racism still exists and is running rampant in our country; a special word of thanks to Tommy Lee Hines. Little did I know that your sacrifice and my participation in marches would inspire me to tell our story. I, too want to thank those unspoken heroes who led in this saga, the Rev. R. B. Cottonreader, Clem "Doc" Peoples, Larry Kirk, Alfonzo Robinson, Steve Wynn, James Guster, John Anthony Rice, Danny White, Marvin Dinsmore, and countless others, I haven't named. Special thanks to The Honorable U. W. Clemon, thank you hardly seems enough.

Prologue

Today, as I tell this story, a worldwide pandemic called Coronavirus or COVID-19, has alarmingly invaded our nation. The deadly virus with no vaccine or immediate cure spread like wildfire and has killed thousands. States issued mandatory shutdowns. School doors closed. Businesses locked up. Restaurants discontinued eat-in dining. Gatherings for church services ceased. Even professional sports ended abruptly. Only "essential workers" were allowed to remain open, manning grocery and drug stores, hospitals and other health care facilities. Life as we knew it prior to this deadly disease came to a sudden halt.

Just as our nation was emerging from the safe at home orders, reminders of another horrible disease plagued our country. This time it was nothing new. It was the age-old deadly disease of racism. On May 25, 2020, Minneapolis police arrested a black man, George Floyd. The 911 caller had stated that Mr. Floyd tried to purchase a pack of cigarettes with a counterfeit $20 bill. Police pulled Floyd from his car, hand-cuffed him, and at one point threw him on the ground. One of the white officers, Derek Chauvin, held his knee on Floyd's neck for eight minutes and 46 seconds. The black man pleaded at least twenty times, "I can't breathe." Onlookers videoed the entire lynching and urged police to let him up so he could get air. With blood trickling from his nose and urinating in his pants, life slowly left his limp body. George Floyd, 46 years old, was dead. Our country, people of all races came together in protest of this horrific display and disregard for life. Marchers by the millions, worldwide, took to the streets in protest of this egregious act of racism. There have been so many other acts of injustice against African Americans which brings me to this story.

For decades, accusations of black men raping white women were a catalyst for violence in our nation's history. Unfair presumptions jeopardized the lives of countless innocent men.

Not many people will remember Decatur, Alabama as a frontline for Civil Rights. Nor will they remember the aggressive means it took to confront the issues of prejudices and inequality occurring in 1908, with the lynching of Tom Stover; in the 1930s with the retrials of the Scottsboro Boys; the gunning down of James Royal; and much later, in 1978 the case of a young, black, intellectually disabled man. Those turbulent times extend into our society today. They illuminate both the courage and continual struggles of African Americans.

During the spring of 1978, Tommy Lee Hines was arrested. With a mental capacity of a young child, surely the evidence would prove him innocent of the assaults. While the majority of the city knew that the charges were absurd, cynical, and almost comical, once again the assertion that the dignity of white southern womanhood had been assaulted. Some years earlier, punishment for such a crime would have resulted in death.

Even though the preponderance of evidence established it was impossible for the accused to commit these crimes, race and racism perpetuated hate and anger. And then, war broke out when a surge of what many called outside interference invaded the town. A confrontation between the black community and the Ku Klux Klan sparked tremors of violence and hostility. Was Tommy Lee Hines destined to be the fall guy to improve community relations and change the city for the better? Or was it Tommy Lee Hines' misfortune to become a victim of injustice, Decatur's sacrificial scapegoat?

CHAPTER 1

A Disturbance

"Oh Lord, leave me alone. Oh Lord, my God, you leave me alone, I ain't doing nothing. Leave me alone."[1]

The culprit's demeanor was a bit off. Fidgeting, his body swayed backward and forward in a steady motion, as he rung both hands in a rhythmic circle.

The streets in the peaceful River City bustled with morning traffic as people hurried in every direction. Various hues of blue brushed the skies of the sunny spring day. It was late May. The white and pink flowers from the dogwood trees were practically gone. Pallets of violet, pink, and red-colored azaleas decorated yards. Pungent fragrances of honey suckle, blossoming hedges and rose bushes hung in the freshness of a mid-morning breeze. Shadows cast by the buildings bobbed as individuals rushed in and out conducting their affairs.

Inside the Morgan County Press building, Barbara Woods busied herself, answering and receiving telephone calls and directing other communications of the day. Out of the corner of her eyes Mrs. Woods spotted a dark figure with deep seated eyes peering inside the building. His hands were cupped around his eyes as he pressed his face against a window pane.

Without warning, the calmness was shattered.

"A black man is peeping in our window," Mrs. Woods screamed into the phone. Within minutes, a wave of police rushed to the building where the perpetrator was seen. After giving a description of the man, the complainant and her co-worker watched through her office window as police scoured the vicinity.

---

[1] (Hines v. State, 1980)

Shortly thereafter, a suspect was located just across the street at the Automatic Screw Company. Officers Keith Russell and Charles Busby rushed through the double glass doors and into the lobby that served as an entrance to the building. Inside, a small reception area was lined with chairs.

Sitting near the door, a young man was engrossed in filling out a job application. He moved awkwardly in his chair, swaying from side to side, holding his pencil tightly, as he marked the paper.

Officer Keith Russell immediately recognized the alleged offender who lived in the Old Town Community. Russell was a big man, standing over six feet tall. He had been assigned to the area some months earlier and knew many of the neighborhood folks. Approaching the man, believed to be the peeper, and without a word, Russell snatched the application from his hand and examined it. Scribbled in almost every empty space on the paper, the hand-writing was large, block, rickety letters, like that a young child might make.

> Name: *"TOMMYINESH."*
> Other training: *"509M."*
> Present employer: *"509M."*
> His employer's address: *"509DdA."*
> Title: *"509DbM."*

Upside down, on the backside of the page, was written *"509MDdiNESH."* [2]

"Tommy, would you mind stepping outside for a moment and talking?" asked the detective. The young man looked at him, but didn't say anything. Grabbing his arm firmly, the tall husky officer rapidly fired questions at the detainee. Because of the alleged offenses, Russell immediately read Hines his constitutional rights, "in phrases."[3] Tommy's fear-stricken eyes stared intently. As police frisked him and loaded him into the backseat of the car, his head was barely visible from

---

[2] Ibid.

[3] Ibid.

the outside. A thick metal grid-like structure separated the suspect and the men in blue.

Hurrying to the building across the street, officers pulled the suspected peeper out of the patrol car and rushed inside. Clutching his arm, one of the policemen pushed him forward, and asked Ms. Woods and the other woman.

"Is he the one?"

"Yes," Woods answered, claiming that the curious fellow visited the office the day before, looking for work. "We don't have any jobs," the woman had told him.

In custody, Tommy Lee Hines said nothing. He was hauled away to the city jail. Russell radioed ahead, "I have a ten-fifteen, J.W."

It was May 23, 1978.

CHAPTER 2

Profiled

Affectionately known in the community as "Brother Tommy," Hines was born in 1952, in Decatur, Alabama. His parents, Richard and Bessie Hines, and five siblings lived in a large red brick, two-story apartment at the subsidized Cashin Homes housing projects. Inside the neat, modestly furnished living room, a chair and couch were next to each other. Ladder back chairs with homemade cushions that covered the slat bottoms were perched around the room. Atop the black and white television set, a bent wire hanger jammed in one end of the broken rabbit ears antenna substituted for the missing ear. Sky blue block walls featured framed reproductions of the Last Supper and Jesus. Several family photographs, Tommy's coloring sheets, his Special Olympics Awards, and other recognitions completely filled one side of the wall.

Tommy was a small man, 5 feet 2 inches tall and weighed about one hundred twenty pounds. His skin was the color of cocoa, and his short kinky hair was close to his head. The face of the twenty-five year old man bore a broad smile that exposed even white teeth.

Each day he moved with long strides through the neighborhood, meandering from street to street, clutching his Bible and nodding his head. Grinning, he spoke to everyone he saw, "Hi y'all doing?"

If someone stopped him in the streets to chat, before long, he would shyly add, "I go to the Newcomb Street Church of Christ. I was baptized by Brother Robinson."

With an IQ of 35 and the mental mind of a six-year old, Tommy could not read, recite the alphabet, count to ten, identify coins, or say the days of the week in sequence. Well-mannered, Hines attended the Cherry Street School Developmental Center located a few blocks from his house. The center served intellectually developmentally disabled pupils.[1]

Shattering the peace of the quiet town, the troubling news of his arrest rocked the Old Town community in ways that no one could have imagined.

---

[1] The Cherry Street Developmental Center was housed in the old Decatur Negro High School building. Erected in 1924, it was the only high school in the city for blacks. It became Cherry Street Elementary School when grades seventh through twelfth moved to the Highway 20 location in army barracks, from the Courtland Air Base, Courtland, Alabama. Construction on the new high school for blacks was completed in 1954.

CHAPTER 3

Horror

"Oh Lord, Oh Jesus, I ain't did nothing."[1]

Startled by the panic-stricken sobs coming from an interrogation room, the two men who were laying carpet in a nearby courtroom were unnerved. A short time later, another loud groan and scream rang out. Precariously, Eddie Marshall, the younger man, moved in to get a closer look. Nearing the door, he took a quick glance through the window and almost let out a gasp when he saw it was Tommy Lee, sitting in the chair, surrounded by police. The terrified young man appeared agitated. Crying, he rocked continuously back and forth.

"Tell us the truth, tell us!" one of the officers shouted, his voice raging, in an attempt to force a confession.

The carpet installers hurriedly grabbed their tools. Floyd Jones and his assistant jumped into their burgundy colored van, and sped off to the Old Town community. Turning into Wynn's Service station on Church Street, they vaulted out of the vehicle and ran inside. The two men recounted all that they had seen and heard to Steve Wynn and locals who sat around shooting the breeze.

Recognizing a gross mistake had been made, Wynn rushed to City Hall. Sergeant Ward informed him that Tommy was in custody and had been arrested for rape. "Has the boy's parents been told he's here?" Wynn asked.

"They have not – will you go by and let 'em know?" the Sergeant responded.[2]

Leaving the jail, Wynn rushed to the Madison Street home to

---

[1] (Hines v. State, 1980)
[2] Ibid.

break the news to his family. Mr. Hines was outside, tinkering under the hood of a car. His apple cap was slightly cocked to one side of his head. He wore old, faded blue overalls and a long-sleeved plaid work shirt underneath. Hearing the most frightening news a parent could imagine, they both raced inside the Hines' house.

The moment they opened the front door and walked inside the residence, Mrs. Hines knew immediately, something dreadful had happened. She was a stay-at-home mom who often took in laundry from neighbors to supplement the family's income. Sporting black plastic framed glasses, the woman was dressed in her usual patterned house dress. Her feet were stuck in a pair of slightly worn house shoes. Tangled gray hair escaped from the printed green and tan scarf that was fastidiously knotted at the forehead, and hugged her weathered, chocolate-colored face.

"What is it?" she asked, looking at her husband.

On hearing the news, the young man's mother let out a soul-wrenching scream, "Lord have mercy! Lord have mercy!" In agony and disbelief, heavy tears flooded her eyes and rolled down her cheeks and onto her dress.

A bit later, Mr. Hines, other family, and local leaders stormed into the police station, insisting they had arrested the wrong person. The charge was shocking. There was no way that Tommy had raped any women. "My boy doesn't go anywhere but to the Cherry Street School and to church," Mr. Hines reasoned. The officers explained to the father, who was prevented from seeing his son that Tommy had been charged with robbery and raping three white women.[3]

---

[3] Historically, black on white sexual assault allegations were a catalyst for violence and racial tensions. August 21, 1933, when the Scottsboro Boys Re-Trials (nine innocent black youth falsely accused of raping two white women) were about to resume in Decatur, Alabama, a white woman reported she had been attacked in broad, open daylight by knifepoint. Police immersed themselves on the predominantly black community with barking blood hounds. An arrest was made. In a night of retribution, sixteen-year-old James Royal was gunned-down after delivering medicine to Dr. Winston H. Sherrard on Vine Street. On Oct. 13, Tom Brown was convicted and sentenced to die in the electric chair at Kilby Prison for the crime. The day before he was scheduled to die, Governor Miller

Billy, an older sibling, received news that Tommy had been arrested. Leaving his job, he rushed to the city jail. Blurting these were false charges and that his brother was "retarded," he demanded to see Tommy Lee. He, too, was prohibited from seeing the inmate.

"The best thing for you to do is leave, or you'll be locked up, too," Sergeant Ward snapped.

Day after day, police refused to allow him to see his brother.

Tommy Lee Hines' arrest sparked impromptu meetings among Old Town's residents in North West Decatur. After a few phone calls were made, it wasn't too long before a racially integrated group of Mental Health supporters and others gathered at a cozy house on Fourth Avenue North West. The yard was neat. Vibrantly colored plants and shrubs filled the flower beds. Inside Mrs. Catherine Garth's house, the sizable living room was packed and people spilled over into the small kitchen. Spearheaded by Marvin Dinsmore, the group discussed the accusations, Tommy's well-being and strategies to get him out of jail. Suggestions to seek assistance from national civil rights organizations, possibly the National Association for the Advancement of Colored People (NAACP) or the Southern Christian Leadership Conference (SCLC) were proposed. This would be the first of many meetings.[4]

Later that evening, Mr. Dinsmore telephoned Ernestine Elliott. The two had served on an interracial board together and he wanted to get her support. About dark, he dropped off cash to secure an attorney.[5]

Mr. Dinsmore had known Tommy Hines since 1969. His daughter and Hines were students at the North Central Alabama School for Developmentally Disabled. He served as chairman of the board at the school, president of The Arc of Morgan County, The Arc of Alabama, and president of the Mental Health Association Board. Knowing Tommy's mental capacity, Dinsmore, who was white, was appalled at this egregious injustice and used his personal resources to assist with the legal defense fund and post bond.

---

commuted his sentence to life in prison. Brown always maintained his innocence. Ten years later, he was paroled.

[4] (Guster 2019)
[5] (E. B. Elliott 2020)

Anger and frustration engulfed the North West community, triggering leaders to hold a mass meeting, two days later. Mrs. Maggie Holmes offered the Newcomb Street Church of Christ for a meeting place. The small house of worship, where Brother Tommy was a member, was full to capacity. Following heart-felt congregational singing and praying, the pastor, Bro. Alfonzo Robinson, informed the crowd that attorney Henry Mims would represent Tommy Lee. Mims services had been engaged by a committee that consisted of Steve Wynn, Marvin Dinsmore and Al Robinson.

Henry Sanford Mims was a native of Mississippi. He received his law degree from the University of California and had re-located to Huntsville, Alabama, around 1974. Mims was known in Decatur. In 1977, he had been retained by a Concerned Parents Committee. The group consisted of both black and white families, who were disturbed that their children in the northwest Austin High and Middle School districts would be bussed across town to Decatur High and Oak Park schools. The United States District court sided with the parents, not the Decatur Board of Education.[6]

The defendant was accused of three interracial sexual assaults and a robbery. Of course, the rape charges were the most serious. It was clear, too, that this manifestation of injustice added to the rage of blacks. Holding their composure, the leaders spoke calmly in an attempt to quiet the people so they could discuss the next course of action.

"Call the mayor," someone shouted.

"We need the NAACP," screamed another.

"Contact SCLC," somebody bellowed at the same time.

The Southern Christian Leadership Conference (SCLC) was contacted. Established by Dr. Martin Luther King, Jr, the African American Civil Rights Organization was established during the Montgomery Bus Boycott.

A Greyhound bus rolled into the station on Grant Street. One by one traveler's dislodged. A handsome tall and slender tan-colored man

---

[6] (Victorious Blacks Set New Goals 1977)

in his forties was one of the last to disembark. He sported an afro and a skinny mustache. The bus pulled off. Curiously, one of the committee members thought, "Could this be him?" The man wore a light-colored shirt, blue denim jeans and matching jacket. A large silver cross hung from his neck, to about the middle of his chest. Walking assuredly, the man picked up his suitcase and strolled toward the three-person welcoming party. Extending his hand, he introduced himself, "I am Rev. Richard Cottonreader, SCLC."

Three days after Hines arrest, the SCLC responded to the alarming call for help. Cottonreader, a project director, was dispatched to Decatur. He had been in Gadsden, Alabama working with another civil rights issue.

As soon as the entourage got into the waiting car, they briefed Cottonreader on the Hines arrest. Within a couple of hours, plans for a mass march were underway.

CHAPTER 4

The Rally

May 30, 1978, the caption underneath a picture on the front page of the *Decatur Daily* newspaper read: "SOME 500 BLACKS PROTEST THE ARREST OF RETARDED MAN IN MARCH TO CITY HALL MONDAY."[1]

The enthusiasm was electric. News of a march brought out masses of people. By 10:30 on that Monday morning, the Newcomb Street Church of Christ was packed. People sat, crammed tightly together on the wooden plank pews. Every inch of standing room was occupied. An encroaching number of concerned citizens stretched outside the double doors, down the steps and surrounded the small house of worship. The massive group overflowed into the front and back yards of neighbors and side streets, adjacent to the church. Many of them discussed what it would take to get justice for Tommy and engaged the widely circulated rumor that John Nettles, SCLC President of the Alabama Chapter, would be attending.

Half an hour late, around 11:30 a.m., Rev. Cottonreader strolled up to the podium and welcomed the group. The chorus of Negro spirituals, freedom songs, prayers, and up-raised hands, roused the audience and seemed to empower them.

Next, rising from his seat in the pulpit and urging the crowd on, Al Robinson proclaimed in a loud voice, "We are somebody! We are somebody! We are somebody!"

The people gave a thunderous applause. Rousing the assembly, someone shouted, "We're ready to march!" The packed house joined

---

[1] (Field 1978)

in. Over and over, they demanded, "We're ready to march! We're ready to march!"

"Whatever we do, we will put God first. We are somebody!"[2] Almost in a chant, Robinson shouted again over the voices of those gathered, "We are somebody!" Cheering and clapping their hands, the crowd showed their approval.

"We don't want any incidents," the preacher said, reminding the gathering activists that the march would be nonviolent. Agreeing with the proposition, a number of individuals in the audience invariably nodded, while some gave a verbally affirming "Amen."

But then, in a subtle shift, Robinson announced, "I know we are ready to march, but our leadership (SCLC) wants to try another tactic first. One thing is for sure, we have a movement here in Decatur. You have more power than you realize."

The Reverend John Nettles was the next to speak. He wore a conservative suit, tie and white shirt with expensive looking cufflinks. Rousing the crowd, Nettles spoke in an authoritative voice, "All nonviolence forces within the SCLC are at your fingertips." Advocating a system of equality for social and economic justice, he referenced the indisputable discriminatory tactics used to keep African Americans from obtaining jobs and equal pay, spotlighting Decatur. "We are just as competitive as anybody in the world, if given a chance." His words resonated deeply at the very heart strings of those in attendance.

After that, Robinson stood again. "We have come here to see Hines exonerated. We'll stay as long as it takes, until he is free. The last thing Decatur wants is a march downtown." Further explaining that the leaders would be meeting with the mayor at 12:30 that afternoon, Robinson asked the mass group to remain at the church until they returned. He, Cottonreader, Nettles, and a few others slowly plodded their way through the mass of people, shaking hands as they exited the building. Once outside, they got into a black Lincoln. The large sedan wound its way through the crowd, down Vine Street, and headed downtown.

---

[2] Ibid.

Nearly, two years earlier, Bill Dukes had been elected mayor of the city of Decatur. The Kentucky native's slogan was "Let's Build For Tomorrow – Together." He had a friendly face and was tall; his dark hair was sprinkled with gray. Having been in city politics for several years, Dukes had earned a reputation of being fair. At City Hall, discussion with the mayor and the city council president, however, had proven unsuccessful in getting an early preliminary hearing for Tommy Hines. The city leader informed the committee that the Hines case was a legal matter and out of his hands. Dukes did however agree to consider a list of grievances from the black community and consented to allowing a march, promising police protection.

Back at the church, after a disappointing meeting with the mayor, the delegation announced to the waiting assembly, "We're gonna march." Adopting SCLC's principles, men front and center, then women and children, it also signified the acceptance of a non-violence approach. Hundreds of outraged protestors poured into the streets. They moved toward Vine Street singing freedom songs and chanting, "Free Tommy Lee! Free Tommy Lee! Free Tommy Lee!" Passing houses and businesses, marchers called out for others to join them, "Get in line brother – we're marching to turn Decatur around today." Scores of people dropped what they were doing to walk with the demonstrators. Some carried signs that read: "Justice"; "Free Tommy"; "Down with Injustice"; "Let's March on City Hall"; "Keep the Faith Tommie." Crossing the railroad tracks, the mass of people passed the little office where one of the attacks occurred. They continued down Bank Street and to City Hall steps. The line seemed unending.

Witnessing the largest demonstration ever in Decatur, police in cars, on foot, and motorcycles observed the marchers.

Arriving at the doors of City Hall, approximately 500 Hines supporters covered the lawn, flooded the streets, and blocked traffic. "We are somebody! We are somebody! Whatever we do, we will put God first. We are somebody!" echoed Al Robinson. Generating more excitement, John Nettles vowed, "This isn't the end of marching in

Decatur. We will keep on marching."[3] Urging justice for Tommy Hines, the peaceful demonstration ended with more singing and praying. The marchers returned to the church, invigorated with a sense of victory.

Watching from his office window, the city leader pondered what would happen to his city.

Nothing appeared unusual when the municipal building opened their doors Thursday, June 1, at 8 a.m. It all changed, however, when demonstrators appeared. Arriving a little after lunch, a silent protest got underway. Marchers carrying home-made signs in support of dropping charges against Hines paraded in front of the Lee Street building. Individuals going in and out of city hall walked nervously. Many of them looked straight ahead to avoid the eyes of the protestors. The black community rallied behind the activists as they bombarded the mayor's office with a barrage of phone calls. As a result, City Hall's switchboard was tied up for hours. Before leaving the municipal building, the group shouted out with a continuous flow of chants "Free Tommy Lee! Free Tommy Lee! Free Tommy Lee!" Returning to the church, they sang civil rights freedom songs.

That evening, under Cottonreader's direction, a local chapter of SCLC was organized. Larry Kirk was elected president. Strategic meetings were held daily at the Newcomb Street Church, which had become SCLC headquarters for the newly formed Morgan County Chapter. The group discussed what worked well and what didn't work. They talked over march strategies, men lead out first, women and children, then cars. They hashed out plans for their next move.

"The pocketbook!" someone screamed. "That's the only way they are going to hear us is we hit 'em in the pocketbook."

Demonstrators were showing up everywhere throughout the day. Tactics of weekly protest, demands to free Tommy, and aggressive approaches attracted more participants and triggered discussion with "the powers that be." Visiting Mayor Dukes' office several times a week, black community leaders continued to press him to drop the charges against Hines. He insisted each time that he had no authority in

---

[3] Ibid.

judicial matters. "It's in the hands of the courts. All I can do is hope that justice is served," he told them. The movement shifted to the business districts. Protestors promenaded in front of stores at Decatur, Gateway, and Westgate Shopping centers, carrying signs that read, "Free Tommy Hines," "Equal Pay," and "Don't Buy Where You Can't Work." It was the first time that the marchers publicly acknowledged that they had a dual purpose: justice for Tommy and grievances against the city.

On June 6, Hines, his attorney Mims, and nearly one hundred Hines allies crammed Judge Rudolph Slates' courtroom for the felony exam. The alleged offender was charged with raping three white women and robbing one. Bond was set for $25,000. Protestors returned to the Newcomb Street Church to discuss the next course of action. According to a *Decatur Daily* article, Ray Nixon, City Council president, agreed that they had no power to get involved; the issue was with the state court. "We cannot interfere with this matter," he contended. Blacks held a rally that evening at City Hall.[4] George Allen, Sr. and Will "Nick" White, Sr. led in prayer.

Extending the protest to Point Mallard Waterpark on June 10, about 150 marchers showed up at the entrance. "Free Tommy Hines" leaflets were passed out. After a couple of hours, demonstrators returned to the provincial SCLC headquarters on Newcomb Street. Detailed suggestions for another march on Point Mallard were considered. "What we need is something that will make a huge statement, hit them where it hurts, in the pocket book," someone in the crowd insisted. Deciding they would occupy Point Mallard again, another person in the audience exclaimed: "We need some mules like the protest with Dr. King." Veronica Mays spoke up. "My uncle has mules and a wagon; he may let us use his." Cottonreader, Kirk and Ms. Mays visited Mr. Percy Goodloe's farm at Wheeler.[5]

Approximately one week later, a two-mule team slowly led the large caravan. *Clop, clop, clop* went the sound of hooves hitting the pavement. The wagon inched alone down Sixth Avenue to the Point Mallard Water

---

[4] (C. D. Wahl 1978)
[5] (Cable 2019)

Park. The assembly occupied a grassy area in front of the park entrance. SCLC had used mules before, during the march on Washington and in a march shortly after Dr. Martin Luther King, Jr. died. The mules were symbolic of poor people and the poverty experienced in the South.

The Justice for Tommy Hines encampment was a sight. Marchers spread their blankets on the ground and pulled out coolers with food and drinks. Children laughed, played, and rode the mules. Adults talked and played card games. Patrons moved quickly in and out of Point Mallard, never saying a word to the protestors.

"Do you know the names of these mules?" one of the leaders asked.

"That one over there is Mayor Dukes, and this one here is Chief Self," one of them sarcastically answered.

Vigils continued. Cottonreader and other protestors pitched tents on the City Hall lawn. The encampment was called "Justice City."

CHAPTER 5

Blame

News of a black man loitering in a white neighborhood and rapes had buzzed in the community. With all the evidence, Hines' mental capacity, his inability to comprehend questions authorities asked, and the fact that he was taking the mood disorder drug, Selective serotonin reuptake inhibitor (SSRI) –a drug that would reduce his libido; had there really been a big break in the cases? Could it have been a case of mistaken identity? Did the presence of the Klan and the cross burning at Delano Park incite the DA to act swiftly?[1] Was Tommy Lee Hines the man to blame, the perfect scapegoat?

On June 22, the preliminary hearing was held. The courtroom was packed to capacity, including Hines' family members, teachers, and supporters. Spectators also stood against the walls and spilled out into the hallway. The first witness, a Southern Railway clerk, said she was attacked at her office on Vine Street, near the depot, on February 16. She testified that her assailant had a plastic bag over his head, but his face was uncovered. According to her, the attacker was slender, 5-feet-6-inches tall, and talked forcefully, cursing.

"Point out your assailant, if he is in the room," Morgan County District Attorney Mike Moebes said loudly.[2] Scanning the room, the woman directed her eyes to the man sitting in front of her, raised her hand and pointed to the defendant. The defense attorney crossed.

The next two witnesses said that they had been apprehended in

---

[1] The Decatur Daily, June 21, 1978, reported that a cross had been burned at Delano Park. Signs in large letters read "Save the Land, Join the Klan" and "Mayor Look, If You Can't We Can."

[2] (Whal 1978)

front of the Wells Street Post Office. One said that the alleged defendant carried her to a place near Amoco Chemical, a plant, just off Highway 20 where she was robbed. The other said she had been apprehended and taken to a house where she was assaulted. The man had used a screwdriver to remove audio equipment from her car. Two of the women identified Hines; the third said she was unable to recognize him.

One of the arresting officers, Keith Russell, said Hines matched the description of a suspect wanted for rape. "A black male, approximately 5'6" to 5'7", 19 to 23 years of age, rather closely cropped hair, clean shaven and a full mouth of [prominent] white teeth."[3]

Russell stated that he did not read the defendant his constitutional rights "in one phrase" and did not read the "whole thing" at one time but "asked him in between those phrases like anything you say will be used against you in Court."[4] According to Russell, the defendant waived his constitutional rights to remain silent and to request an attorney and admitted to raping three women.

Mr. Hines, the father of the accused, swore, "That boy don't go nowhere except to the Cherry Street North Central Alabama Developmentally Disabled Center and Church of Christ on Newcomb. Those police are wrong." Others who testified on behalf of Hines were: Alfonzo Robinson; Maggie Holmes; Cora Daily, a neighbor; Tim Dunlap, a teacher-supervisor at the Decatur Adult Center; and Marvin Dinsmore.[5] All testified to their knowledge of the degree of the defendant's mental retardation.

The following day, June 23, 1978, district attorney Mike Moebes quietly called a special grand jury. They returned indictments accusing Thomas Lee Hines on three counts of rape, charging that he "forcibly ravished" the following women - Rosemary H., Lorene M. and Sharon W. One of the accusers said $400 in denominations of twenties had been taken and a charge of robbery was also included. Judge Slate ordered a

---

[3] (Hines v. State, 1980)
[4] Ibid.
[5] Ibid.

psychiatric evaluation and, without the knowledge of Hine's attorney, a secret transfer to Bryce Hospital in Tuscaloosa was arranged.[6]

The black community was outraged; just another reason not to trust the system, they claimed. How could authorities move the prisoner without informing his counsel? Mims said the DA called and asked him to bring his client to the courthouse. When they arrived, the commitment order already had been signed by Judge Richard "Dick" Hundley.[7] Hines bond was revoked and he was taken back into custody.

Citing several breaches, the attorney for the accused filed a writ of *habeas corpus* with Judge Hundley. He asked that his client be returned to Morgan County. The commitment denied the defendant "due process," and was a violation of his 14th Amendment rights,[8] Mims stated.

The black community was absolutely furious and outraged that Hines had been secretly taken away. Focus now was clearly on seeing that no harm came to Brother Tommy. In previous times, a hallmark of Jim Crowism was that police pretended to release a black prisoner, kill him, and then invent a story that he was trying to escape. Fury and fear propelled more people to join the demonstration. Churches were contacted and people went from door-to-door to solicit funds to further Hines' defense.

Within hours, two sheriff deputies delivered Tommy Lee Hines to Bryce Hospital at Tuscaloosa, where he was committed to the mental institution for a psychiatric examination.

That Friday evening, enraged protestors gathered at the Morgan County Courthouse, demanding to see the DA, Mike Moebes. "He's gone for the day," Sheriff Van Ward told them.

---

[6] The Alabama Insane Hospital was established by the Legislature as the Alabama Insane Hospital in 1852, on a tract of land east of the University of Alabama campus, in Tuscaloosa. The hospital opened in 1861 and was later renamed for Dr. Peter Bryce, the first superintendent, who had helped established the asylum. (Morton 2019)

[7] In 1962, Richard L. Hundley was appointed as Circuit Solicitor for 8th Judicial Circuit representing Morgan, Limestone and Lawrence counties. He became a circuit court judge in 1969 and held that office until retirement in 1994.

[8] (Field, Lawyer for Hines Challenges Order Sending Him to Bryce 1978)

Cottonreader eyed him and then turned and spoke to his followers, "He has betrayed our trust." Looking back at the sheriff, the SCLC field representative announced, "We're not moving until Moebes is here."[9]

"Taking him out of here without our knowledge is just wrong, an unfair and unjust act," declared Kirk. "We are going to see justice done. We're not moving, until Moebes come[s] out and talk to us!"

In protest, about 75 picketers with food, pillows and covers spent the night in the courthouse lobby on the first floor. Authorities from both the city and county observed them. Demonstrations continued through the weekend. That Saturday about dusk, dozens of protestors showed up on Castleman Street at the District Attorney's house. Even though Moebes' house was dark, the party gathered on his front lawn. Annoyed that the DA would not come out, or was gone, protestors filled the street as they sang and paraded down the southwest thoroughfare. Neighbors peered out of their windows. Some of them quickly switched their lights off and called police. Officers rushed into the neighborhood and ordered the group to disperse or be arrested. The dissenters left.

Demonstrations continued that Sunday. Disrupting the quiet, around 8 p.m., Cottonreader and about 150 marchers, including some new faces, plunged onto Mike Moebes' property again, just as they had the previous evening.[10] The DA's front yard was filled with people milling around. They flowed onto the sidewalk and into the street. Some sat on the curb. The group chanted and sang. To the tune of the old Negro Spiritual, "Satan, We're Going to Tear Your Kingdom Down," they caroled, "Moebes, we're going to tear your kingdom down, Mr. DA, we're going to tear your kingdom down." Neighbors disturbed about the crowd's presence and the noise called both the police and sheriff's departments. Arriving at the scene, lawmen jumped out of their cars. Scanning the group, Police Chief Pack Self quickly shouldered himself through the crowd, and headed toward Cottonreader. In a brusque commanding voice, he announced, "Get moving, clear the area

---

[9] (C. Wahl, Hines is Indicted Moved to Tuscaloosa 1978)
[10] (Department 1978)

or you'll be taken directly to jail." Waiting for a reaction, he warned, "If you return you will be arrested."[11]

Up until then, the black demonstrators were ignored. Early Monday morning, June 26, Hundley ruled that blacks could no longer congregate on courthouse property. He alleged that courthouse business was disrupted due to their presence. Effective immediately, the order was signed by both Hundley and Judge Thomas Coggins.[12] The latter had been elected 8th Circuit Judge in 1972. Years later, his unsavory judicial career ended with a conviction related to drugs.

As soon as the order was signed, deputies were tasked to man all entrances to the courthouse. The order stated in part: "Persons who fail to show the officers securing the building that they have specific business with the circuit courts or offices located in the building shall not be allowed in." Entrance into the courthouse was left to the discretion of Sheriff Agents.

Met by armed deputies equipped to enforce Hundley's ruling, Cottonreader and the protestors were denied admission when they attempted to go into the building. Sergeant Henson read the order to Hines' supporters and then handed Cottonreader copies of the court order and court docket.[13] Spewing rage at this latest news, demonstrators turned, went outside and stood near the entrance of the courthouse steps and doors. They watched as every African American attempting to enter the premises was asked, "State your business." Eventually, the marchers was asked to comply with the order and leave. They did.

Back at the church, a large group was called upon to protest this action at an evening rally. Hundreds gathered at the courthouse. After singing, praying, and speeches on the unfairness of the treatment of Tommy Hines, Cottonreader burned the court order, prompting cheering roars. Afterwards the activist group returned to the church.

A couple of days later, on June 28, a small white car pulled up in front of the Morgan County Courthouse shortly after 1 p.m. John

---

[11] (Field, Lawyer for Hines Challenges Order Sending Him to Bryce 1978)
[12] (Department 1978)
[13] (Sheriff 1978)

Anthony Rice let out three passengers who quickly made their way inside the building. Cottonreader was the first to go in.

> Sergeant Cook: *What is your business at the courthouse?*
>
> Cottonreader: *I am a citizen of the United States and reside temporary in the Morgan County jurisdiction and have three or four stops I'd like to make.*
>
> Sergeant Cook: *State your business.*
>
> Cottonreader: *I don't see any reason why I need to have an escort, police escort.*
>
> Sergeant Cook: *If you don't have business in the courthouse, I am going to have to ask you to leave. Either state your business or leave...unless you have business, we deny you entry to the Courthouse.*
>
> Cottonreader: *I didn't come as a demonstration... I came with a couple of personal friends of mind, and I don't intend to back off. I would like that understood, I came in a spirit of non-violence...I got God with me.*
>
> Sergeant Cook: *Do you refuse to leave?*
>
> Cottonreader: *That's right.*
>
> Sergeant Cook: *Your [sic] under arrest. Come on.*[14]

A younger man with a pink hand towel slung around his neck, wearing jeans and a brown, long-sleeved shirt followed. As soon as he stepped inside the door, a deputy posed the same question. "Do you have business in the Courthouse?"

"Personal business," Kirk said testily. "I am a citizen of Decatur, Alabama, and have been all my life...I am a citizen of the United States my father and my mother lived in this City all their life, my grandmother, my uh, uh grandfather, all my brothers and sisters have grown up in this city. We have a right to enter the courthouse at anytime and anywhere, I have not seen in the Alabama Constitution..."[15]

---

[14] (Sheriff 1978)

[15] Ibid.

"You're under arrest; come on," said the officer.

The man at the door cast his eyes on June C. Ford. A light-skinned woman with hazel eyes, her sandy hair was in cornrows and gold hoop earrings dangled from her ear lobes. Small in stature, she weighed about 110 pounds and stood about 5 foot 6 inches tall. Right away the woman spoke, "I am a citizen also; I do have business here."[16] After providing her address and answering a series of questions from the officer, she, too, was taken into custody and booked into the Morgan County jail.

Nearly two hundred protestors gathered that night to show their objection to the arrests and moving Hines secretly. Attempting to talk over the crowd a couple of the speakers spent time pleading with fellow-marchers to remain non-violent. As with each rally, participants crossed arms, linked hands, sang songs, and swayed.

The next day was a scorcher. About fifty blacks left the Newcomb Street Church. The sweltering sun was high and beat down on them. Searing heat radiated from the sidewalk. Beads of sweat rolled down their faces. Several of the marchers wore hats to shield their heads from the hot, humid day. Many carried wet towels to refresh themselves during the mile walk to the courthouse. Others had dry towels slung around their neck or suspended from their belts to wipe sweat. Some even wiped perspiration with their sleeves. All the while, they sang and chanted.

Arriving at the courthouse, Hines' supporters attempted to gain entrance through the double glass doors. A confrontation ensued as law enforcement wielding billy clubs fought to push the blacks back. Cursing and sneers increased hostility. More arrests followed. Police dragged the most vocal ones, Danny White, Jack Kirk and others, on the front line inside the building. White warned, "Whatever you want to do with *me* is all right." The crowd outside the doors shouted, "Us." "When I go into custody, there'll come some more," he warned. Danny White had participated in most of the marches and was a neighbor to the Hines' family.

"There'll be more of us, you'll see," said Kirk. "You can't arrest all

---

[16] Ibid.

of us." Hurling themselves forward, picketers linked their arms as a human chain, and attempted to sit in the outer doors entrance. Kirk and White were arrested.

After posting bond, Cottonreader met with the sheriff and later promised that there would be no demonstrations from June 30, until after the Fourth of July.

March on Morgan County Courthouse
June 28, 1978 SCLC Members and Hines' Supporters
Courtesy: Morgan County Archives

July 8, 1978 - SCLC Chapters March
Top. *L-R*: The Rev. John Nettles, Dr. Joseph Lowery
Courtesy: Morgan County Archives

March on Decatur - June 9, 1979
Bottom. SCLC Members and Hines' Supporters
Courtesy: Morgan County Archives

March on Decatur - June 9, 1979
SCLC Members and Hines' Supporters
Courtesy: Morgan County Archives

Scapegoat

March on Decatur - June 9, 1979
March to City Hall: Klan Rally Counter-demonstration
Courtesy: Morgan County Archives

CHAPTER 6

God's In-Crowd

As hot air balloons soared in the sky at the first Alabama Jubilee in Decatur, high flying tempers soared as well.

On July 5, Cottonreader, Larry Kirk, and June Ford appeared in Court. All three were charged with Section 13-5-4, Resisting Officer in Execution of Process. Each one was fined $500 and sentenced to six months in jail.

A number of demonstrations had been planned to correlate with SCLC's annual meeting in Birmingham. A larger crowd was expected and a bigger meeting place was needed for the keynote speaker, Dr. Joseph Lowery. A Huntsville, Alabama, native, Lowery had been selected as the third president of SCLC, in succession of Dr. Martin L. King, Jr.

On July 7, Dr. Lowery's distinctive preacher's voice stirred the waiting congregation at the historic First Baptist Church.[1] In his empowering speech, he thundered, "You in here are Decatur's and God's in-crowd. Decatur will never be the same because you will never be the same." Waiting for the applause to quiet, the articulate leader continued, "Don't you think the way black people in Decatur are treated doesn't affect black people around the world?" Amid booming cheers, loud shouts and amens, the assembly of more than 500 agreed. Fired up, the leader continued, "We're not going to fight just for Hines; we're going

---

[1] The church had been founded a year after the Civil War. It was a small replica of the Sixteenth Street Baptist Church in Birmingham, where a September 15, 1963, bombing occurred, killing four young girls and injuring fourteen. The building was designed by Wallace A. Rayfield, the second licensed black architect in the United States.

to fight for black policemen. We're going to fight for black firemen. We're going to fight for black people on the City Council. We won't stop now." He urged local clergymen and black professionals to join in the "Free Tommy Hines" movement. "There can never be any rest in our hearts until Tommy Lee is set free," he contended. "And right now, our main concern is seeing Tommy free." [2]

The next day, hundreds of demonstrators lined up. Leading the march were: the Rev. Joseph Lowery, SCLC president; Mrs. Evelyn Lowery; the Rev. John S. Nettles, SCLC state president; Dr. Nelson Smith, SCLC vice president; the Rev. Cottonreader; local leaders, Kirk, White, and the Rev. Robinson. Arm in arm, they began the mile-long march to the courthouse. Also participating were SCLC members from across the United States. By now, blacks from all over Decatur had joined the movement. Those who had previously shied away from the interest group for fear of losing their jobs, or other reasons, united and marched to the county government building.

To get a better view, the leaders in the rally climbed the steps to the second floor portico. The stirring orator, Rev. Lowery, gave an arousing appeal. "I want to ask the intellectual part of the community – where are you? And what about the religious part of the community, the preachers, the deacons, the trustees-where are you? There can never be any rest in our hearts until Tommy Hines is set free!"

Numerous requests to meet with District Attorney Mike Moebes were repeatedly ignored. Blacks stepped up their game and demonstrated two, three, and sometimes four times a week.

On Friday, July 14, Sheriff Van Ward's car pulled into his designated spot at the county courthouse. His passenger, Tommy Hines, had been released back into the county's custody and found competent to stand trial. A $25,000 bond was posted, and Hines was free to go home with his parents.[3]

---

[2] (Wahl 1978)
[3] (Hines Out on Bail, Declared Competent 1978)

CHAPTER 7

The Move

Gun-toting Klansmen were in full regalia, wearing white hooded, funnel-shaped headgear and long white robes with red and white circled patches. They, along with hundreds of others, surrounded the ghastly image of a fiery twenty-five to thirty-foot cross.

Founded shortly after the Civil War, the Ku Klux Klan consisted of many former Confederate soldiers, who organized to retain white supremacy in the South. Confederate General Nathan Bedford Forrest was the first grand wizard. Cruelty such as floggings, burnings, tarrings and lynchings were common responses to those who challenged Jim Crow laws. In Decatur, the Columbian Union, Sovern Klan of the World, was organized on April 5, 1919. Members included 60 leading white men in Morgan County.[1] From the late 1800s through the African American Civil Rights movement, the society was known for terrorizing people of color to keep them in their place.

Activists continued their efforts to free and save Tommy Hines. Escalating conflicts between blacks and whites spiraled. Like a phoenix, the Klan rose out of its dust on that July day. Alarmed by black demonstrators and the erection of SCLC's tent city, the organization said their objective was to help the mayor and the town's judicial system keep order.

The July 15, 1978, membership rally created a celebratory environment. Traffic was horrifyingly congested.[2] Arriving early for

---

[1] (Columbus Union Names its Officers 1919)
[2] More than a thousand attended the Klan membership rally. Dues for the Decatur organization was $3 per month and the fee split between the national, state and local group. (Scott-McLaughlin, Bailey and Torres-Frankel 1984).

the 7 p.m. meeting, hundreds of cars lined up along the Beltline and Alabama Highway 24 intersection and branched off onto almost every side street.

The balmy hot air reeked of fuel. Country music, food, and a variety of drinks – including alcoholic beverages – contributed to a county fair atmosphere. Estimated at more than a thousand spectators, the grassy grounds were jam-packed as the swarm of jubilant white men, women and children gathered around the gigantic cross, which was wrapped in burlap and soaked in coal oil. Some sat on blankets or lawn chairs while others stood, all smiling, laughing and having a good time. Several carried weapons. Masses of people also lined the streets watching from old pick-up trucks, cars, and station wagons. Car doors were stretched wide opened, and children were perched atop car roofs, while parents rested on top of the hoods. All had come to hear the message of Bill Wilkinson, Imperial Wizard of the Invisible Empire, Knights of the Ku Klux Klan, and to view the colossal cross burning.

Standing in the back of a flatbed truck, Wilkinson was dressed differently from the others. He too wore a white horned hat that fell to his shoulders, but his flowing white robe adorned with KKK insignia had blue stripes on each arm. He wore a blue belt around his waist; and a blue scarf was around his neck. Wilkinson was surrounded by his captains who carried semi-automatic weapons. He told his listeners that the Klan was there to "support the local judicial system, as it decides Tommy Hines' fate."

"I'm not saying that Hines is guilty, and I'm not saying that he is innocent," Wilkinson added. "But I am saying let justice flow in Decatur."[3] The rain started, as the cross blazed. The flames burned orange with streaks of blue and reddish colored fire. Sparks popped and spit as they cascaded out and downward. Grayish-blue smoke rose upward as the rain began to fall harder.

At the same time, refusing to be intimidated by the symbol of fear and violent times that many would rather forget, about 150 blacks

---

[3] (Fields and Morgan, Over 1000 Watch Klan Burn Cross 1978)

marched, arms linked together, to the courthouse and down Second Avenue. "The Klan thought we wouldn't march because they were in town, but we don't give a damm about the Klan," said Cottonreader.[4]

Throughout the blistering hot summer, numerous counter demonstrations took place. In mid-August, anxieties and heated tempers further inflamed the community. Observing his city being consumed with hatred must have been unsettling for Mayor Dukes. He saw blacks marching and singing freedom songs. He witnessed robed Klan members camping out opposite the blacks. He looked at the Klan armed with vicious dogs, baseball bats, chains, big sticks, and guns, swearing not to leave until the city addressed SCLC's tent city. The opposing groups were less than twenty five feet from one another. He watched the two groups throwing jabs of insults, rancorous curses, and an occasional shove. The gentle man contemplated how to get a grip on the chaos that had consumed his beloved city.

Undeterred, the black protesters marched twice that day. At a demonstration earlier, they prayed, made speeches, and sang freedom songs. "Remain peaceful," their leader warned. Someone in the mix broke out with a mantra, "We want the wizard, we want the wizard, we want the wizard," suggesting that Imperial Wizard, Bill Wilkinson come forward. Others joined in.[5] Wilkinson did not acknowledge the chant.

Mission accomplished and led by police escort, the blacks returned to their Newcomb Street base. On the way back, amid insults, two men on conflicting sides were embroiled in a brief grapple near Ferry Street. The faceoff fueled fears of a disturbance. Back at the small meeting place, Cottonreader warned, "All they want is one sign of violence, and we're dead. Leave your tempers at home. I hope we grow from this experience today."[6]

That evening, Mayor Dukes left his house just in time to witness

---

[4] Ibid.
[5] (Field, Klan Members Burn Cross at City Hall: Blacks March 1978)
[6] Ibid.

white men and women with their children, even babies, gather for the Klan demonstration.

Around the same time, hundreds of SCLC activists approached the municipal building. Just as they passed the Klan, a man started singing the civil rights anthem, "We Shall Overcome." Loudly, in unison, they chorused, "We're fired up. We're fired up. We're fired up." Like the booming of a cannon, a woman whose smooth, dark brown skin glistened with sweat, hollered, "Ain't Gonna Take No More." At the top of their voices, the crowd joined Mrs. Beauty (Viola Lane) in the refrain, "Ain't gonna take no more. Ain't gonna take no more." Regardless of Cottonreader's instructions, some individuals anticipated trouble and armed themselves. Speakers addressed the large assembly and reminded them of the goals of their non-violent movement.

Dukes, other city officials, law enforcement, and numerous others watched as the Klan again burned a cross and sang "Dixie" on the city hall lawn.

Earlier that week, a white woman, Annie McDouglad, had been shot and killed in her home. Employed by the Community Action Agency, she'd earned a reputation for helping blacks. Three weeks prior to her death, the shape of a cross had been burned in her front yard. On August 11, SCLC laid a wreath in her honor at city hall.

City ordinances were quickly drawn up to shut down tent cities by banning them and other such assemblies from all city properties. Decatur Council President Thomas Counts, and Councilmen Jack Allen, Ray Nixon, Phil Raths, and James Roberts unanimously approved the ordinance.

The encampments were vacated and pulled down because of the ordinance. A small discoloration of grass was the only visible sign of the tent cities.

On Tuesday, August 15, a busload of about fifty national and state civil rights leaders rolled into Decatur on a chartered bus. The SCLC leaders had been in Birmingham attending their 21st Anniversary Conference. This was the third meeting in Decatur that hosted iconic civil rights leaders; this time the Rev. Ralph Abernathy, co-founder of SCLC, was present. A major civil rights figure, Abernathy and Dr.

Martin Luther King, Jr., were cohorts on the forefront during the civil rights era. Abernathy was a close adviser to Dr. King and a key leader during the Montgomery Bus Boycott. He relinquished his role as SCLC National president in 1977, a year before the Hines saga.[7]

Nearly 200 marchers arrived outside city hall. Addressing the group, Larry Kirk, Morgan County's SCLC President, thanked his fellow associates for supporting Tommy Lee Hines. "They look at you as outsiders; we look at you as brothers and sisters," he said. The next person to speak was Dr. Lowery. In his masterly voice, he blared, "We may not raise much money in Decatur, but we definitely will raise a lot of hell until things are right." The crowd cheered as Ralph Abernathy spoke passionately. He promised to give all the support the Decatur chapter needed. Abernathy shouted, "You are not alone. You are not alone."[8] After about thirty minutes, demonstrators returned to the church where further discussions of the Free Tommy Hines campaign were held. Visiting SCLC members departed for Birmingham.

The day after the big march, Attorney Henry Mims filed a Change of Venue request, citing pre-trial publicity. He specified that his client "could not receive a fair and impartial trial based on his race and the demonstrations, rallies, and overnight camps that had polarized the community along racial lines."[9]

Noting that it would be nearly impossible to find an impartial jury, Judge Hundley granted the motion to move the trial to Cullman, the next county over. The order was signed August 18, 1978.

Cullman County's population was approximately 14,200. Of these, only 1 percent was black. At the time, only two black families lived in town. The remaining African Americans inhabited an area in Hanceville called the Colony. Highly upset that Hundley would even consider moving the case to Cullman County, Mims argued in a controlled voice that Hines could not receive a fair trial there either.

Historically, the city of Cullman was known as a "sundown

---

[7] (Editors 2020)
[8] (Field, Civil Rights Leaders March on City Hall; Abernathy Pledges Support for Hines 1978)
[9] (State of Alabama vs Tommy Lee Hines 1978)

town."¹⁰ Old timers remembered disturbing experiences while riding the Greyhound bus through Cullman. The driver would ask black passengers to pull the curtains because whites would throw tomatoes, eggs and rocks at the windows where black travelers sat. Others told stories of a painted sign that read on entering town, "Niggers Don't Let the Sun Go Down On You In This Town."

To reflect an adequate racial makeup, Mims requested that the change of venue be rescinded and sent to either Madison or Jefferson counties. Judge Hundley rejected the request.

---

¹⁰ (Sorin 2020)

Figure 1

STATE OF ALABAMA   IN THE CIRCUIT COURT

MORGAN COUNTY   JUNE TERM 1978

It appears to the Court that certain persons and loiterers have congregated in the vicinity of the Court. These persons constitute a source of interference, and disturbance to the Courts, to the jurors, witnesses and parties, as well as the general public. The following shall be done to insure order.

FIAT

Persons who fail to show the officers securing the building that they have specific business with the circuit courts or offices located in the building shall not be allowed in. The press shall have free access to the courtrooms and all public areas of the courthouse and its curtilage without restraint of any kind. No cameras shall be allowed in any part of the courthouse or its curtilage.

The Sheriff shall strictly enforce all the provisions of this order.

These restrictions shall not apply beyond the present jury term of court.

This the 26th day of June, 1978.

R. H. Hundley, Circuit Judge

Figure 2

Filed In Office
June 30 1978

IN THE
DISTRICT COURT OF MORGAN COUNTY, ALABAMA
STATE OF ALABAMA CRIMINAL DIVISION

WHEREAS it appears to the Court that certain persons have recently congregated at or near the Morgan County Courthouse and their conduct and behavior is such ass to interfere with or disturb the courts, parties, witnesses, officers of the Court, and the general public; now therefore, to insure order and safety during the session and term of court on this date, it is

ORDERED BY THE COURT AS FOLLOWS:

All persons entering the courtroom shall be carefully observed by the Sheriff or his assigned deputies and, in the discretion of the officer, any person within the courthouse or its curtilage may be stopped and searched for weapons or other instruments which may be used as weapons;
In the event a weapon or such instrument is found on any person not a law enforcement officer or officer of the court, the same shall be confiscated by the Sheriff. (Should such person have a lawful permit to carry the weapon or instrument, the Sheriff shall return it upon that person leaving the courthouse grounds.);
Should the courtroom fill to its seating capacity, other persons seeking admission shall be so advised and be denied entry;
Reasonable order is to be maintained in the halls of the courthouse.
Should any person create any disturbance or refuse to comply with the instructions of an officer attempting to execute this order, he shall be denied entry into the courtroom or ejected therefrom and removed from the courthouse premises; or, in the discretion of the officer, such person may be detained until he can be brought before the court whereupon he may be cited for contempt.
The working press and news media shall have free access to the courtroom and other public areas of the courthouse and its curtilage. No cameras shall be allowed inside the courtroom.

Melba S. Dutton

Figure 3

STATE OF ALABAMA
COUNTY OF MORGAN

ORDER

The Sheriff is hereby ordered to prevent any Interference with, obstruction or impedance of the administration of justice during this term of Court. Specifically the Sheriff is ordered to keep the halls and entrances clear of unlawful assemblies of persons or disorderly people during the times of Court is in session the week of June 26, 1978.
Done this 26th day of June, 1978.

Tom B. Coggins
Circuit Judge

Figure 4

August 1978 City Ordinance

Section 16-3. - Camping on public property.

(a) It shall be unlawful for any person to do any camping or to erect or maintain any tent, shelter, trailer, wagon or other type of camping shelter and related equipment on the following:
   (1) The city hall property, known also as the municipal building, located at 402 Lee Street, NE, Decatur, Alabama, and being on that property bounded on the southerly side by Lee Street, on the westerly side by Ferry Street, on the northerly side by Cain Street and on the easterly side by Well Street.
   (2) All public rights-of-way within the corporate limits of the city.
   (3) All city library properties.
   (4) All parks and playgrounds except that such shall be allowed in established or designated camping areas set aside by the director of parks and recreation for such purpose, and subject to all rules and regulations promulgated in connection therewith.
   (5) County courthouse, public office buildings, and grounds of such, within the city, except where such is authorized thereon by constituted authority.
(b) Any personal property referred to in subsection (a) of this section not removed by the owner or custodian of such from the premises mentioned therein shall be deemed abandoned personal property, and shall be handled in accordance with the provisions of section 22-6 of this Code.

(Ord. No. 2147, § 19-57.1, 8-15-78; Ord. No. 2151, § 1, 8-21-78)

CHAPTER 8

Nose to Nose

Not guilty and not guilty by reason of insanity. The plea entered by Henry Mims, who was accompanied by New York Attorney George Hairston, with the National Association for the Advancement of Colored People (NAACP), shocked and infuriated those who congregated in Cullman to support Hines. A disturbing disappointment dominated Kirk's countenance. He called for an immediate meeting with Hines' lawyer. "He is innocent and insanity has nothing to do with it," shouted Cottonreader.[1] Surrounded by Hines' allies, Tommy was escorted out of the courtroom.

Trial was to begin on October 2. The judge placed a gag order on lawyers until jurors were selected.

On Saturday, September 30, Hines' supporters met at the Newcomb Street Church of Christ. A short prayer service, a strategic talk and a reminder of their non-violent movement followed. About noon, thirty or so Hines' backers – women, men and children – left on foot. Leading the group were John Nettles, Rev. Fred Shuttlesworth, Larry Kirk, and R. B. Cottonreader.[2]

A small convoy of cars snaked behind them, moving down Highway 31. Every few miles, police or state trooper cars sat on the side of the road and watched as the procession traveled the 32.9 miles to the Cullman County hall of justice. Occasionally, one of the cars would pull out and trail the marchers, break off, and then another would take its place.

Near Flint, a light-colored state trooper's helicopter appeared.

---

[1] (Plea of Hines Shocks Backers 1978)
[2] (Blacks March For Cullman 1978)

Propellers whirling, the obtrusive thwapping rotor noise hampered the melodic chants as the whirly bird lunged low, hovered, pulled up and circled off. On the lookout for trouble, Trooper Conrad, the man in the bubbled tower of the chopper, could clearly be seen as he methodically performed this routine over and over again, lunge low, hover, pull up and circle. After about five hours, the pilgrimage arrived in Hartselle. Members at Pennylane Church of Christ provided lodging for the night.

On a beautiful fall Saturday, the robin's-egg blue sky welcomed the dozen or so walkers as they continued their journey southward to Cullman. Numbers had dropped; the thirty-two mile distance was far, and many concurred that they would drive over on Monday morning. Before long the invasive racket of the helicopter shadowed them once again.

Smiling from ear to ear, a little girl got out of a car. She lugged an enormous cardboard sign, hung by a thick string, around her neck. The poster enveloped half her little torso and reached down to her knees. Written in large letters across it: *"March to Cullman. Free Tommy Hines. 'God's Child."*[3] Ten year old, Latonya Fuqua was dressed in matching short-sleeve shirt and shorts, her hair was half up and half down. The ponytail in the middle of her head was held in place with a colorful clacker hair bow that complimented her clothing.

A year older and slightly taller than his sister, the boy, Paxton Holyfield, followed close on her heels. His oval-shaped face was framed by a medium, tightly curled afro. He wore brown laced shoes, jeans, and a "Free Tommy Hines" T-shirt.

The small band started this leg of the walk singing:

> *This Little Light of Mine, I'm gonna let it Shine,*
> *This Little Light of Mine, I'm gonna let it Shine,*
> *This Little Light of Mine, I'm gonna let it Shine,*
> *Let it shine, Let it shine, Let it shine.*
> *Everywhere I go, I'm gonna let it Shine,*

---

[3] (Dunnavant, Klansman Met. Blacks Marching in Rape Charge Protest Taunted 1978)

Everywhere I go, I'm gonna let it Shine,
Everywhere I go, I'm gonna let it Shine,
Let it Shine, Let it Shine, Let it Shine.

Anticipating the walkers, several hundred Klansmen and white supremacists lined each side of Highway 31, just south of Falkville, Alabama. As black demonstrators neared the Soul Harbor Church, they heard the hostile cynical taunts, laughs, screams and scornful sneers. The crowd chanted loudly, "White Power. White Power. White Power." A man hollered, "Niggers go home!" Others joined him in the thunderous tune, "Niggers go home, you're not going to march in our town."

Topping the hill, the marchers were greeted by approximately 2,000 whites. A sea of red, blue and white Confederate flags swayed in mid-air. Miles of cars, vans and pickup trucks parked along the side of the road were decorated with the same insignia. Adding fuel to an inferno of rage, the blacks moved closer. The whites shouted louder, hurling insults as they frantically waved Confederate flags.

Without warning, vehicles rushed in and surrounded the blacks. Despite the threat of danger and possible death, they kept walking. About 80 officers, some in helmets and riot gear formed a barrier to force the blacks back and demanded that they turn around. Defiant, Larry Kirk brazenly rejected the command to stop. "I'm coming through!" he shouted. "Shoot me, kill me. I'm not afraid to die because I'm on my way to freedom." A woman in the group screamed. "You should arrest them, not us!" Delois Elliott continued, "They got guns and knives and sticks, we ain't got nothing. We're non-violent and we ought to be able to walk peacefully down a highway in this state." Another person exclaimed, "You can't stop us from marching."

Suddenly, all hell broke loose. An officer shoved Kirk, grabbed his arm and announced in a gruff tone, "You're under arrest." About the same time, sudden, deafening and loud explosions blasted and then smoke. Was it gunfire? "They're shooting at us!" Someone hollered twice. Panic-stricken, the blacks turned, ducked and ran wildly, jumping into cars that were at the rear of their caravan. Taking a few steps back, the men at the front of the line retreated. Tires screeched as the vehicles swiftly backed up, made a U-turn and sped off toward Decatur. It was Sunday, the Lord's Day.

Crippled by the Klan actions and the men-in-blue barricade, Cottonreader vowed that the march was not over. "I don't know when we will get there, and I don't know if I will get there with you." he said. "But my trust is in God and I know he will protect our cause."[4]

Kirk was released a while later. Cullman officials informed demonstrators that they could not march there because of the potential threat of violence. SCLC leaders and Cullman police negotiated an acceptable plan for Monday, they thought. The agreement was, "You can march to the Cullman City Limits. Stop. From that point on, march six feet apart and two abreast."

John Anthony "Satchel" Rice, a neighbor and friend of the Hines family, went to the Hines house the early morning of October 2. Rice and his companion, James Guster, were prepared for trouble. In his early thirties, Guster was a tall, slender, brown-skinned man, with a neatly trimmed mustache. A Vietnam veteran, he was dressed for combat in his starched and ironed, olive-colored military uniform. Guster put his hand on Mr. Hines' shoulder and promised him, "I will die protecting Tommy." Saying goodbye to Mrs. Bessie (Hines' mother), with packed lunches, the men along with Tommy made their way to the family car, an old light-colored Chevy four-door sedan, and headed for the courthouse in Cullman. Once outside, Decatur city limits, Mr. Hines and his entourage drove above the speed limit. Expecting a possible ambush any moment, they had been watchful, and made the distance in record time.

The three-story, white marble structure adorned with slate-blue panels looked inviting, a sharp contrast to the venomous spews of hatred that had welcomed marchers a day earlier. Security was high; officers scanned everyone going into the courtroom with hand-held metal detectors. The car carrying the defendant pulled up and parked

---

[4] (Dunnavant 1978)

into the angular space. Tommy Hines and those with him got out of the automobile. Flanked by his own private security detail, in addition to police and undercover officers who sported handcuffs and holstered guns, the accused was ushered inside the courthouse.

Counter demonstrations between civil rights groups and the Klan prompted national news coverage. Local and national news outlets, including ABC, CBS, and NBC television stations invaded Cullman to cover the highly emotionally charged rape case.

The Presiding Circuit Judge Jack C. Riley banned tape recorders and cameras from the courthouse and even prohibited demonstrations within a block of the building.[5] Riley was a Dale County native and former attorney. The middle-aged man had been appointed Circuit Solicitor in the 1950s by Big Jim Folsom. He now sat on the bench as judge for the 32nd judicial circuit.

The first case before the court was that of Rosemary H., [last name withheld, initial provided], a 21-year old Southern Railroad clerk. Prior to qualifying jurors, Judge Riley said:

> I know that you and I and all of us are under some slightly different pressure than we usually are here…it's when the pressure gets on that the true mettle of the individual comes to the fore. What we are doing today is merely a culmination of…centuries of people trying to live together under rules of law.

Several hours later, an all-white jury of nine men and three women was selected from the venire and sequestered. No blacks had been on the jury roll.

Defense attorneys Henry Mims and George Hairston argued that Hines' did not have a jury of his peers. Judge Riley rejected the motion to strike a new jury.

About mid-morning, Hines' advocates decided it was unsafe to resume the highway march by foot. Supposing there would be trouble,

---

[5] (AP, Blacks March to Trial Falls Back 1978)

they drove to the next county to ensure that the agreed upon plan was adhered to as specified. Exiting their cars at the green and white Cullman City Limits sign, the protesters lined up. Moving forward they sang, "Ain't gonna let no Klansmen turn us around, turn us around, turn us around." At and all around the sign stood robed and hooded Klansmen and a taunting white crowd, including women, who loudly screamed insults and vulgarities. Enthusiastically, the chanting and cheering group waived confederate flags of all sizes while others shouted and held up signs that read, "Keep Cullman Clean, Keep Nigers [sic] Out," and "Nigers [sic] Go Home." Several Klansmen, with arms folded, tried to block the approaching marchers.

Poised for action, a phalanx of law enforcement officers from various departments moved in. Wearing full riot gear, armed with shot guns, semi-automatic weapons, and walkie-talkies, police erected a human wall separating the opposing groups. The line stretched across the highway as officers stood shoulder to shoulder. They were fixed in opposite directions of one another. Some faced the approaching demonstrators. Others faced the jeering whites, who were shouting raucously, and flinging hostile comments such as "Niggers Go Home!" and "Go Home Coons."

The blacks endeavored to plough their way through the threatening crowd. Infuriated and standing nose to nose with the whites, some of them bellowed back. Authorities moved swiftly to gain control of the demonstrators.

"You promised us that we could walk along the shoulders or on the sidewalk and that's just exactly what we want to do," Dr. Joseph Lowery told Cullman Police chief, Roy Wood.[6] Lowery referenced the shared understanding made the day before by SCLC leaders and the police; "march six feet apart and two abreast." "We don't have any band; we don't have any majorettes. We're not making a parade. We're just walking down to the courthouse to be with our brother."[7]

Ignoring the mutual agreement to allow the march and to defuse

---

[6] Ibid.
[7] Ibid.

tension, the police chief arrested SCLC's national and state presidents, as well as twenty-one others, and booked them into jail. All were charged with "parading without a permit."

Shortly after being taken into custody, all demonstrators were released on a $300 bond each. The property bonds were put up by Dr. Lowery. "I don't think I've ever been in any more hostile an environment, not even in Selma or in Montgomery," the civil rights leader said.[8]

When asked about the arrest, a Cullman newspaper quoted state trooper commander, "This action was taken to save a major confrontation. Somebody would probably have gotten hurt." Troopers from Anniston, Birmingham, Tuscaloosa, and Decatur were in Cullman to assist in keeping order.[9]

Spectators settled into their seats inside the courtroom, blacks on one side and whites on the other. A rather unexpected shift occurred when the back door of the paneled third floor courtroom opened. Abruptly, a black man, handcuffed and flanked by law enforcement officers, entered.[10] He had been arrested earlier in the summer for raping an eleven year old. A Decatur detective declared, "Your Honor, I have a man here that's got a confession that will throw a lot of light on this trial." Rising from his seat, the judge banged his gavel twice and announced, "I don't know who you is [sic], you say you are a detective from Decatur, but my name is Jack Riley, and they call me 'Speedy Jack' here. I got a trial going on. This is not a confession court. Get this man out of my court and don't ever show your face in this court no more." [11]

Rumors buzzed.

When court recessed a little after 5 p.m., the judge firmly warned jurors not to read the newspaper or watch the news. "There is Monday Night football [sic] and plenty of love shows to watch," he admonished. The twelve boarded the Cullman County Rescue Squad van that carried them to the Holiday Inn for the night.

---

[8] Ibid.
[9] (Fields, Judge begins Jury Selection; Walk Resumes 1978)
[10] (Morse 1978)
[11] (Guster 2019)

CHAPTER 9

The Trial

On Tuesday morning, the second day of the trial; nerves were on edge and anxieties extremely high. Blacks stayed together. Some went inside the courtroom while several kept a watchful eye outside the building, on the lookout for trouble. Periodically, the surveillance team would change guard. Throngs of white men, many of whom had participated in the undertaking to stop the black marchers, gathered inside the courtroom. Near the east side of the courthouse, some huddled under an enormous pecan tree that became known as the "Klan Tree." They wore jeans, short-sleeve shirts, or T-shirts and caps, some bearing the KKK emblems. Others wore faded bib overalls and a few sported neck ties and dressed in business attire. Several of the men leaned on large sticks that could easily double as weaponry. A number of cars and pickup trucks were parked within a short distance of the courthouse. Some of the trucks were old and rusty, and a number of newer models with gun racks in rear windows, displayed shotguns and rifles, a small number of them with telescopic sights. A two-toned van, its sliding door opened, cruised up and down the streets around the courthouse. A young bushy-haired man with a thick mustache, wearing grubby overalls and work boots, sat on the edge of the seat. Screaming profanities, he swayed a twisted rope in the form of a hangman's noose back and forth.

Later, locals told reporters, "They should never have moved the trial to Cullman in the first place. Shoulda kept it in Decatur. Our blacks had it good. They could come on into town, they could eat where they want and trade where they want and nobody would bother them. But after this is all over and these outsiders leave, it's going to be rough on our blacks."[1] Another said, "We wouldn't mind if the 'outsiders' drove into town in cars like people, but we ain't gonna let them march [into] our town and push the white citizens off our streets."[2]

There was a high level of security, and the courthouse was heavily guarded. All individuals were searched and went through a metal detector as they entered the building. Once inside, Hines was escorted to the defense table. The small man had on brown-checkered polyester pants and a striped long-sleeved, button-down shirt, with a white T-shirt underneath. He sat between attorneys Henry Mims and George Hairston. The mentally deficient man's eyes darted around the room. He slouched in his chair, head bobbing downward with occasional spasmodic rocks. Tommy was conspicuously disassociated from the courtroom drama, clueless about the gravity of his quandary. Hines' supporters, both black and white, sat together behind him. A few white faculty members from Hines' school was in attendance as well.

Sitting at the table with Morgan County's District Attorney, the victim's head was slightly downward. Choked with emotions, she held a crumbled paper tissue tightly in her hand.

Court opened. "All Rise," a voice thundered. The presiding judge, clad in his long-flowing black robe, took a seat behind his massive desk. He rapped his gavel for silence. Judge Jack C. Riley was the presiding justice. The charge was read and a plea was entered.

Assisting Mike Moebes, Morgan County DA, was Julian Bland, Cullman County's district attorney. The prosecution proceeded first with his opening statement, "The state will prove that Hines raped this woman."[3] At the close of his remarks, he summoned his first witness. The young lady was medium-built, with thick, reddish-brown hair and in her twenties. She stood and raised her right hand.

"Do you solemnly swear to tell the truth, the whole truth, and nothing but the truth, so help you God?" asked the bailiff.

Answering in the affirmative, "I do," she sat down. Describing her

---

[1] (Whites in Cullman Angry About Trial 1978)
[2] Ibid.
[3] (AP, Hines Raped Her, Woman Testifies 1978)

ordeal, the railroad night clerk testified that she was assaulted about midnight on February 16, at the railroad depot. It was bitterly cold.

"He had a green garbage bag tied over his head…like a lady's scarf," the woman said, insisting that she could see her attacker's face through an opening in the bag.[4] The witness divulged that around 8:30 p.m., she had driven a short distance and then exited her Pinto to inspect the track. Suddenly, her assailant ran toward her, grabbed her and pulled her back onto the freight dock and into a room in the warehouse. Recalling the violent act, and with tears in her eyes, she said her perpetrator asked, "You think you're too good to kiss a black person?"[5] The victim also stated that she offered her assailant money if he would leave her alone.

"Is the man in the courtroom?" Moebes asked.

Jurors looked intently in the direction of the plaintiff. Arm stretched out, she pointed confidently at the defendant. "That is the man," she said firmly. "I resisted at first, but he pulled my left arm behind me and said in a gruff speaking tone, 'Don't or I'll break your arm.'"[6] The woman said that the man also took ten to twenty dollars from her purse and warned that he knew her name, where she lived, and where she worked.

"You're telling a fat ass lie, you're telling a lie!" an elderly black lady, Mrs. Ida Mae McDaniel, stood and shouted in a fiery outburst of emotions. The judge slammed his gavel for order and threatened to clear the courtroom if there was any other improper actions.[7] Those sitting next to the aging woman attempted to calm her down.

For the young mentally underdeveloped man to commit such a horrific act was unconceivable. Mrs. McDaniel was certain of that. A defender of Hines' since his arrest, she was fondly referred to as the grandmother of the Tommy Hines movement. Mrs. McDaniel had attended all or most of the meetings and demonstrations. A native of Selma, Alabama, she often boasted about marching with Dr. Martin Luther King, Jr. and the Reverend Ralph Abernathy.

---

[4] (Morse 1978)
[5] Ibid.
[6] (AP, Hines Stands Trial for Rape in Alabama 1978)
[7] (Elliott 2020)

Under sharp cross examination, George Hairston, co-counsel for the alleged offender, quizzed the witness. It seemed highly improbable that she could positively identify Hines as her attacker. The victim admitted that her perpetrator's head was concealed with a green garbage bag. There had been no line up, and when police showed her the five photographs prior to the June preliminary hearing, she did not pick out the defendant.

> Hairston: "It was easy to say it was Tommy Hines, wasn't it?"
>
> *Woman:* "He was the one who raped me."
>
> Hairston: "No ma'am. That's not the question. It was easy to identify him sitting there with those white people, wasn't it?"
>
> *Woman:* "Yes Sir."[8]
>
> Hairston: "Did you kick or struggle?"
>
> *Woman*: "He was very strong. He had so much power."
>
> Hairston: "Are you saying this is the man that was so strong?"
>
> *Woman*: "Yes sir, that is the man," she pointed.[9]

A physician who examined the victim shortly after the assault testified about her injuries and medical condition.

Defense counsel filed a motion to suppress Hines' alleged confession, maintaining that it was coerced, involuntary and that based on the developmental disability of the accused, he could not understand the Miranda Warning.[10] The jury was dismissed while the judge listened to testimony as to the competency of the alleged confession.

---

[8] (Dunnavant, Alabama Rape Confession Recalled 1978)

[9] (Burns 1978)

[10] Miranda Rights were created in 1966 as a result of the United States Supreme Court case of Miranda v. Arizona. The Miranda warning is intended to protect the suspect's Fifth Amendment right to refuse to answer self-incriminating questions. (Miranda Rights 2020)

Officer Keith Russell was the second witness to take the stand. Under oath, he said that on May 23, the department received a call about a peeping tom. According to him, Hines matched the description of a rapist, so they took him in for further questioning. He was thorough in reading him the Miranda Rights as they drove to city hall, he told jurors, "You have the right to remain silent. You have the right to an attorney...." Revealing details of that day, Russell said he radioed Detectives Doyle Ward and Robert Clark and told them he had a suspect in custody, "I worded it ten-fifteen, J.W., that means I have a prisoner in custody, someone that they needed to talk with."[11] The defendant had admitted to three rapes, Russell told them.

> Russell: "Tommy, keeping in mind what your constitutional rights are, why don't you get it off your chest, it is bothering you."
>
> Hines: "I know."
>
> Russell: "When was the last time you went to the post office?"
>
> Hines: No response.
>
> Russell: "When was the last time you went to the post office?"
>
> Hines: "Six weeks."
>
> Russell: "What did you do with the can?"
>
> Hines: "I threw it in the garbage."
>
> Russell: "How many women have you raped, two or three?"
>
> Hines: "Three."[12]

When the trial convened on Wednesday, white observers outside the courthouse perimeter had gathered early. Periodically, they would attack the blacks by yelling foul language and offensive racial insults.

The defendant was heavily guarded.

---

[11] (Hines v. State, 1980)
[12] Ibid.

Testimony continued about the admissibility of the ostensible confession.

Court recessed for lunch. As soon as the blacks were outside the courthouse, once again groups of white men screamed obscenities at them. A Ford truck honking its horn, with a sign that read "Niggers Ease On," circled the courthouse block once, departed, and then made the loop a few more times. Leaning out of the windows, occupants wildly unleashed cursing and racial rants. A squad car wheeled in front of the truck and blocked its path. Police emerged from nowhere and surrounded the men in the pickup. They arrested the driver, Steven Reeves, and his brother. Later, Steven was "charged with disturbing the peace, resisting arrest, driving with revoked license, carrying a concealed weapon, and possession of marijuana." His younger brother was not indicted.[13]

Following the expert witnesses, Mr. Richard Hines, Sr. father of the accused, was called to take the stand. He was decked out in a three-piece suit, paisley tie, and a large light-colored apple cap. Addressing the competences of his son, Mr. Hines told the court that he "could not read or write or ride a bicycle.[14] I tried to learn [sic] him how to ride a bicycle, but he couldn't do that." Mr. Hines revealed that his son did not speak until he was seven years old.[15] "He never sassed or said a harsh word to me or to his mama in his life. He never went out [of the house] late at night and can print only a few letters but is unable to read, write or tell time."[16]

The pastor of Newcomb Street Church of Christ was the next witness. Brother Alfonzo Robinson praised Tommy Hines for his love of the church, his faithfulness, and regular attendance. He told jurors, "Tommy is retarded." The minister couldn't remember a Sunday when the defendant was not in church. Since his member was afraid of the dark, he often picked him up and drove him to the church so that he wouldn't miss Sunday or Wednesday services. Eager to attend church

---

[13] (Dunnavant, Alabama Rape Confession Recalled 1978)
[14] (AP 1978)
[15] (Donnavant 1978)
[16] (UPI, Threats Interrupt Retarded Man's Trial 1978)

services, Tommy would invariably stand at the door, cuddling his Bible as he waited for his ride. Alluding to his intellectual abilities, "Whenever Tommy helped serve the Lord's Supper, a lot of times in going from point A to point B, he would have to be coached."[17] Robinson said.

Mockingly, Moebes asked: "Does Hines smile a lot?"

"Yes," Robinson remarked.

"But you wouldn't know if he smiled while raping someone?"[18] the DA sarcastically remarked.

Before he could answer, a man rushed into the courtroom and handed the judge a note. The message read, "There is a **BOMB** in the courthouse set to go off in three hours!"[19] Riley stood and announced, "Court is adjourned for lunch until 2:30. Leave the courtroom quietly please, ladies and gentlemen. Vacate the courthouse building, all of you, and leave the courthouse curtilage. Anyone remaining in the courthouse or courthouse grounds will be forcibly removed."[20] Once the county courthouse was vacated, police, sheriff and state troopers methodically searched the three-story building for nearly an hour from bottom to top. A second bomb threat was directed to the courthouse, but this call came to the sheriff's office sometime after the building was emptied. *The Montgomery Advertiser* reported that the county's chief law enforcement officer said, "The search was made more as a precaution than in expectation of finding an explosive." The calls were a hoax.

Shortly after the bomb threat, Judge Riley held an impromptu press conference clarifying his position on a motion to dismiss the trial or for a change of venue. He walked out front and announced, "If and when we get to that point (of an unfair trial), I assure you the appropriate action will be taken. I'm a human being too."[21] Mims and Hairston had filed the motion citing prejudicial pre-trial publicity. Without informing defense attorneys first, Riley rejected the motion using the public platform.

---

[17] Ibid.
[18] (AP, Bomb Threat Clears Court in Cullman Rape Trial 1978)
[19] Ibid.
[20] (Burns, Bomb Calls Delay Trial; Court Security Tightens 1978)
[21] (AP, Hines Judge Stress Impartiality October)

Court resumed for the afternoon session. The defense called several individuals who attested to Tommy's mental capacity. With the jury out, Dr. Jack R. Anderson conveyed that after examining Hines on three separate occasions, the man's mental retardation range was moderate with a mental age of six years and four months. Anderson, a Professor of Psychiatry at the University of Alabama's School of Medicine, affirmed, "At very best, his best level, he was never able to operate intellectually above an I.Q. of between 35 to 45 at his very best."[22] When Attorney Mims asked if the defendant was capable of understanding his legal rights, the psychiatrist stated, "This would be much beyond the ability of anyone who is moderately retarded. There would be no way at all he would understand it."[23] Dr. Anderson further testified, "No, I don't believe he had any chance in the world of understanding them (Miranda warnings); as far as waiving them, he would think that was something you did with a flag, waiving in the abstract sense, he would never be able to understand that concept."[24]

Mrs. Maggie Holmes stated that she was never able to teach Tommy to read and write. "He would only repeat what I said." He never was able to hold a pencil straight."[25]

School officials said he was a good student and didn't give them any problems.

Cora Daily, a neighbor, remembered the first words Hines uttered at seven years old: "Ol Cora." Describing his abilities, she gave examples of his functional impairments and struggles. Mrs. Daily was also a member of the church that the accused attended. She, too, would often pick him up for services.

Arguments continued on whether to allow evidence of the confession.

On Thursday, the testimony of Dr. Ferris O. Henson, another expert witness for the alleged offender, was given in the absence of the jury. Dr. Henson was an Associate Professor of Special Education at Alabama A&M University, Normal, Alabama. His testimony concurred

---

[22] (Hines v. State, 1980)
[23] (Hines Incapable of Understand His Legal Rights 1978)
[24] Ibid.
[25] (UPI, Threats Interrupt Retarded Man's Trial 1978)

with that of Dr. Anderson. Henson explained that "Mentally retarded individuals usually respond very positively toward authority figures," like the police.[26] Henson stated that Hines could not have understood his constitutional rights to remain silent, even if the Miranda had been read ten times. Due to the defendant's cognitive limitations, he would go along with anything anyone said; Tommy was "susceptible to suggestions." The *Decatur Daily* reported Dr. Henson testified that the defendant was unable to think in the abstract. "When I say, 'shake a leg,' you know I mean hurry up. But a retarded person would react by interpreting it literally. He'd probably shake his leg."[27]

In his professional opinion, Dr. Henson said, the defendant was "trainable." "Someone who is operating at Tommy's level can be expected to learn a few self-help skills – bathing, going to the bathroom alone, and general grooming."[28]

Under cross, the prosecutor attacked Dr. Henson's credibility, demanding that Hines was "faking both his mental and physical capabilities."[29]

> Henson: "I doubt that anyone functioning at Tommy's level would know what a constitution is, let alone of the implication it included."
>
> Moebes: "Hypothetically, if Tommy was to go down to the freight department with police, show them where the victim's car was parked, which door was entered to commit the crime and describe the details of the crime, what would that indicate to you."
>
> Henson: "If that was the case, I would think Tommy Hines would not be the person in custody. Hypothetically that could not happen."

---

[26] (Hines v. State, 1980)
[27] (C. D. Wahl, Hines Said 'He Had Sex' - Consultant 1978)
[28] (Cantrell 1978)
[29] Ibid.

Moebes: "Well, would you please accept the hypothetical fact that it did happen? Anyway, the fact that he did do that, what would that indicate?"

Henson: "That type of behavior would not be typical of someone functioning at Tommy's level."

Moebes: "Then, if it did happen, you would have to say that Tommy Hines has more ability than has been assumed, that Tommy Hines would be an entirely different person than you have indicated to us today?"

Henson: "Then hypothetically, I would have to say yes."[30]

Henson further stated that Hines lacked the ability to describe details of the rape because of his IQ. "It doesn't fit," he told Moebes. He added that the "sex drive diminishes at a lower IQ." Judge Riley then inquired about the sexual ability of an individual with such intelligence. The witness replied, "It has been observed that as the IQ goes down so does the sex drive."

"Then everything would be the same but to a lesser degree?"[31] the judge asked.

"Probably," Dr. Henson responded.

Seemingly removed from the proceedings, Tommy Lee Hines sat as he had on other days with his head down, sporadic rocks, and on occasion he would dab his eyes dry.

Joel Loftin, a psychologist with the Alabama Department of Mental Health at the Lurleen B. Wallace Center, knew Tommy from the Cherry Street Developmental School. He testified that "he rarely showed aggressive tendencies, that he could count to about six and he was seldom absent."[32] He discussed Hines spirituality and told how he "delighted in talking about his being baptized and accepted as a member of the church. He had learned some ideas of love and forgiveness that go

---

[30] (Dunnavant, Psycologist's View Sought. Witness Challenged in Rape Trial 1978)
[31] (C. D. Wahl, Hines Said 'He Had Sex' - Consultant 1978)
[32] (Cantrell 1978)

back to his church training." Loftin told the court, "He had a spiritual maturity I haven't seen in normal individuals."[33]

When Marvin Dinsmore took the stand, he described the defendant as a kind individual. "He was very personable, smiling, friendly, and easy going."[34] Dinsmore, a white man, was among the first to campaign for Hines' release and provided financial support for his defense.

Friday morning, a rebuttal witness for the state testified. Dr. Thomas Smith, Jr. was a lawyer, psychiatrist and consultant for Bryce Hospital and was a member of the panel that declared Hines competent to stand trial. The doctor established that the young black man had a "clear view of right and wrong." He added, that during questioning, Hines, admitted, "They say I stole some money, and that I did some other things wrong. I sure am sorry. I didn't mean to do it."[35] He further divulged that Hines disclosed that he forced himself on a woman "one time" at a railroad depot.[36]

> Moebes: "Do you feel that he understood or would understand what he was doing if he waived those rights and made a statement to the police officers on May the 23rd, 1978?"
>
> Hairston: "Objection, Your Honor."
>
> Judge: "Overruled."
>
> Smith: "Yes, sir, I believe that he would, at the level, if it was put the way that you are stating it, but, not the reading of it."
>
> Moebes: "Not the reading, if it were read to him orally by a police officer?"
>
> Smith: "And explained in the sense that you just..."
>
> Moebes: "You are misunderstanding me, if the Miranda Warning was read as I am reading them to

---

[33] (UPI, Rape Trial Continues 1978)
[34] (C. D. Wahl, Hines Said 'He Had Sex' - Consultant 1978)
[35] (Taylor 1978)
[36] Ibid.

you, read to him, he doesn't read them, they are read to him by a policeman?"

Smith: "I think he could understand."

Moebes: "You said a few minutes ago that they must be explained?"

Smith: "I heard that they were explained."

Moebes: "You heard?"

Smith: "Yes. Let's assume they were not explained to him, I would say that [sic] could be put to him in such a way, read coldly, using only those terms, there might be a borderline case in that situation, if they were read and not explained."

Moebes: "Now, say that again."

Smith: "I said if they were read without any explanation, without any modification, it might be difficult for him to understand them word for word as you were putting them, you are taking one word out at a time."[37]

On re-cross, Dr. Smith deduced that in his opinion there was no evidence that Hines could not function sexually.

Friday evening both sides rested their argument on the motion to quash the confession.

---

[37] (Hines v. State, 1980)

CHAPTER 10

"It Doesn't Fit"

On Monday morning, October 9, when court opened, Circuit Judge Jack Riley announced, "The defendant knowingly and wittingly [sic] gave up his rights to remain silent."[1] Admitting the alleged declaration into evidence, he agreed with the prosecution, "The jury has the authority to decide whether this confession has credibility."[2] After the ruling, he also noted, "It is obvious we have had outside incidents, but it is also obvious that we have done everything in our power to assure a fair trial in this courtroom. ... While it's unfortunate these things occur, we have to live with them, and since these incidents did not occur at the courthouse, they do not affect the trial."

A week of closed testimony was provided to the judge by detectives, expert witnesses, and others, without the jurors present. The jury returned to the courtroom. Presenting its first witness, the state once again called Decatur policeman Keith Russell to the stand. He recounted the events leading up to Tommy Hines' arrest on May 23 and the so-called confession. He informed the court that after receiving a call about a man peeping in a window, police had apprehended a suspect at the nearby Automatic Screw Company. At the time, the man was completing an application. According to Russell, Hines fit the description of a reported rapist. "A black male, approximately 5'6" to 5'7", 19 to 23 years of age, rather closely cropped hair, clean shaven and a full mouth of [prominent] white teeth."[3] Needless to say, the description didn't fit. During a physical examination while at Bryce

---

[1] (AP, Dozen Witnesses Likely to Testify on Hines' Behalf 1978)
[2] (Dunnavant, Confession Account Gets Judge's Nod 1978)
[3] (Hines v. State, 1980)

Hospital, the defendant "weighed 143 pounds, had a height of 5'2", and was 25 years old."[4] Russell stated that when the women pointed Hines out as the Peeping Tom, police placed him in the rear seat of the patrol car.

The officer further explained, "He was sitting in the car, and I was standing there, and I asked him would you go down to City Hall and talk to two detectives. I remind you again that you don't have to say anything, anything you say can be used against you, you have the right to have an attorney with you and do you understand."[5] Russell made clear to the court that he "most certainly" would have let Tommy leave, if he had asked.[6] While riding to the station, the prisoner became agitated. Admonishing the alleged offender to get whatever was troubling him off his chest, the patrolman interrogated him. "How many women have you raped, two or three?"

"Three," the respondent had said, according to Russell[7] The *Decatur Daily* reported that the officer acknowledged "prior to questioning Hines, police knew of only two rapes."[8] Russell also disclosed that he read and explained Hines the Miranda Rights and that he understood them.

The job application was submitted into exhibit.

Next, the prosecutor called Sergeant Doyle Ward to read the accused's signed-written, voluntary confession.

"Objection!" Henry Mims shouted at the top of his voice. With a flustered look, he offered a motion to suppress the so-called statement. Stating grounds for his protest, the defense lawyer insisted that the confession was "coerced, contrived and involuntary." Once again, the magistrate ordered the jury removed from the courtroom so that he could consider Mims' proposal. Attorneys argued about the admissibility and degree of credibility of the confession. A bit annoyed with the New York attorney's aggressive defense approach, stone-faced Riley directed

---

[4] Ibid.
[5] (Hines v. State, 1980)
[6] Ibid.
[7] (C. Wahl, Judge Allows Jury to Hear Confession 1978)
[8] Ibid.

his attention to Hairston and bellowed, "We'll have to send you to law school yet."[9] Overruling the defense's motion, the judge allowed the jury to hear the written confession.

On Tuesday morning, Sergeant Ward testified that when Russell arrived at the station with the prisoner, Hines was turned over to him and Sergeant Robert Clark. Clark read the prisoner his rights, specifically, "You have the right to remain silent, and anything you say could be used against you in a court of law!" According to Ward, "Sergeant Clark asked Mr. Hines if he understood his rights, and Hines said he did, Sergeant Clark then asked Mr. Hines if he understood he didn't have to talk to us, he had the right to have an attorney present."[10] Hines said he did [understand], and at 10:35 a.m., waived his rights, and printed his name in large twisted letters, "TOMMY iNESH."

During the interrogation, the sergeant and Clark took Hines to the scene of the alleged attack. "When we drove up, Mr. Hines stated that was where the girl worked."[11] While inside the warehouse, the officer conveyed, "I asked Mr. Hines to show me where he had attacked the girl, and he looked around and whispered, he didn't know."[12] Returning back to the police station, Tommy was booked into jail around 11:45 a.m. On further interrogation about another assault, the detective revealed that the alleged perpetrator forfeited his rights to having an attorney present. Hines signed another waiver around 1:30 p.m., "TOMMY iNES."[13] Later, detectives procured another confession, wherein Hines allegedly admitted to a second assault. The oral statement, written by police, was signed by the defendant at 3:25 p.m.

Ward then read the purported affirmation of guilt, stating that it was in Hines' words:

> I, Tommy Hines, am 25 years of age and my address is 509 Madison St. Northwest. I have been advised and

---

[9] (Dart, Cullman, Alabama feels Trial of Textbook Southern Justice: 1978)
[10] (Hines v. State, 1980)
[11] (Cantrell, Hines Defense Begins 1978)
[12] Ibid.
[13] (Hines v. State, 1980)

> duly warned by Doyle Ward who has identified himself as a Decatur policeman of my right to the advice Of counsel before making any statement...I hereby waive my right to the advice of counsel and voluntarily make the following statement...About two or three months ago I was out walking and I went by the train station and got a drink of water. While I was there I saw a girl that I knew worked there. After I got a drink, I went outside and waited for her to come out. While I was waiting I found a sack and put it on my head. I saw the girl come out...I went up to her and grabbed her...I forced the girl to a building. After we got in the building I unsnapped her pants and pulled them down...After I got through with the girl, I left and went home...[14]

While Detective Ward read the purported confession, the victim's eyes moistened, tears streamed down her face. In silence, she patted her eyes dry with a handkerchief.

In a familiar but most unwelcomed scene, the atmosphere in the courtroom was like a sharp-edged knife. Tensions further intensified as Judge Jack Riley repeatedly sided with the prosecuting attorney. Time and again, he "sustained objections to the defense's questions and overruled objections to the state's questions."[15]

Under cross examination, defense attorney Hairston ripped into the detective.

"Are these the defendant's exact words?" he asked.

Ward responded that most of the sentences were answers to questions that the officers had asked. He affirmed that the elder Hines was denied the opportunity to see his son when he was first arrested.

Calling police policy into question, the defense counsel asked, "Is it police procedure to prevent relatives from seeing those in custody?"

---

[14] (Dart 1980)
[15] (C. Wahl, Witnesses Testify Hines' is Innocent 1978)

"There is a visiting day, police procedure." Ward quipped, "There are exceptions though."

"Was this an exception?" Hairston inquired.

"It could have been,"[16] Ward scoffed.

Hairston was unrelenting in his questioning.

"Were you aware of the facts contained in Hines' alleged confession before you took his statement?" he questioned.

Ward replied that he was somewhat familiar with the account from a report he'd previously read.

"Is it policy of the Decatur Police Department to tape confessions?" pressed the defense lawyer.

"It has been done," the witness stated.

Hairston queried, "Did you know the defendant could not read?"

"He said he could read a little," the detective said.

"Did you read the statement back to him after you had written it?" probed the defense attorney.

"Yes, he stated that the statement was correct after I read it to him," Ward replied.

"At what point did you ask him about raping black women?"

"He said he hadn't raped any, he had a girlfriend," the investigator admitted.[17]

After more questioning, Detective Ward stepped down. The questionable confession and photographs of the train depot were entered as evidence.

The state rested about 4 p.m.

Defense attorneys quickly filed a motion for a directed verdict on grounds of lack of evidence by the state and "the pretrial publicity, threat to blow up the courthouse, and violent atmosphere in which this trial has been held."[18] Earlier that day, the judge had rejected a motion to recuse himself from the case. The NAACP attorney, George Hairston,

---

[16] Ibid.
[17] (Cantrell, Hines Defense Begins 1978)
[18] Ibid.

had argued racial bias against Hines' defense team. Also, for the fifth time, the jurist disallowed a motion for a mistrial and change of venue.

When court ended, lawyers for Hines were asked if they knew what the judge implied by his sarcastic remark regarding "pet names" for lawyers on both sides. Hairston responded, "Yeah, Nigger One and Nigger Two."[19] Riley later denied that he was prejudiced or that he had used any "pet names." The judge stressed that he had only tried to maintain a "relaxed atmosphere."[20]

---

[19] (Dunnavant, Rape Defense Loses Argument. Written Confession Allowed 1978)
[20] (C. Wahl, Hines' Defense Could End Today 1978)

CHAPTER 11

Verdict

Several witnesses for the accused, including experts, relatives, neighbors, and school staff were called again to repeat their testimony. This time it was before the twelve jurors.

All the experts for the defense supported the fact that Tommy Hines was "moderately retarded" and incapable of understanding the Miranda Rights. Repeating his previous testimony, Dr. Ferris Henson, assistant professor at Alabama A&M University (A&M University), said that based on testing, the defendant could not have used the words and sentence structure given in the statement, as police asserted. He stated that an individual with Hines' IQ could not recall "chronological order of events," as outlined in the confession. In his expert opinion, he concluded, "If Tommy Hines had conned the school system and psychologist all these years, it would be possible."

Mike Moebes, the prosecutor cross-examined. "To your knowledge, could a trainable mental retard commit a crime?"

"They have been known to," Henson said.

When the prosecutor asked if they could perform sex, Dr. Henson responded, "They have been known to do so, yes."[1]

Joel Loftin, psychologist at the Lurleen B. Wallace Center, once again gave his opinion of Tommy's mental intelligence. Based on several test results, the defendant's psychological assessment established that "waiving his rights could be confusing," and that the accused would have a mental deficit in "understanding abstract terms."

Questioning the experts professional ability, the prosecutor asked, "Is it not a known fact those tests are not better than the person

---

[1] (UPI, Father: Son Home Night of Rape 1978)

administering the test and evaluating it.[?]" Loftin glowered at the prosecutor. Slightly raising his voice and in a self-assured manner, he answered, "This is one of the most widely used tests of mental ability. I am a competent examiner."[2]

Taking the oath, Dr. Jack Robert Anderson, witness for the defense and a psychiatrist at the University of Alabama's School of Medicine in Birmingham, sat down in the witness box. He spoke in detail about individuals classified at the degree of retardation as the alleged attacker. "It is my opinion that the defendant does not have the capability to understand these proceedings or to meaningfully participate."[3] Anderson further stated, "Nor do I think he could understand the statement (his Miranda Rights)." He noted that people with such low IQs as the respondent are "highly suggestible to authority figures."

Under direct-cross examination, lead defense lawyer, Mims probed for further clarification:

> Mims: "If Tommy Lee Hines was placed in a patrol car with two officers and asked, 'How many women did you rape, two or three?' what would the answer likely be?"[4]
>
> Anderson: "Tommy Lee Hines would have said what he thought they want to hear. I don't believe he understood the question or the consequences of an answer to him."[5]
>
> Mims: "If Hines was placed in jail and interrogated for several hours by two different officers, after being picked up from the streets, having not eaten, denied visits from his father and friends, would Tommy Lee Hines be operating in a stressful situation?"[6]

---

[2] (C. Wahl, Hines' Defense Could End Today 1978)
[3] (Cantrell, Hines Defense Rest 1978)
[4] (Dunnavant, Defense Lawyers Rest Hines Case 1978)
[5] Ibid.
[6] (Cantrell, Hines Defense Rest 1978)

"Yes," the witness declared.[7]

Under cross, Moebes blasted Dr. Anderson about Hines' ability to comprehend portions of the confession. The DA's voice rose high, hurling question after question.

"Would he be able to understand 'I screwed her?'"

The doctor acknowledged that Hines might remember the statement if it were within five minutes after being questioned.

"If he made the statement would you say that your assessment of Hines' capability is incorrect?" Moebes retorted.

"If he made it without prompting," Anderson answered.[8] After a few more questions, the psychiatrist stepped down from the witness stand.

On Wednesday, employees at the Cherry Street School Developmental Center provided information about Tommy's behavior and performance at school. They, too, had previously provided testimony with the jury out.

Tim Dunlap, a teacher and supervisor at the school testified that Hines "was very polite and well mannered, and presented no absentee problems." The teacher stated that the defendant had insisted on going to Vocational Rehab, "And that he said he was going to be like Martin Luther King and stand up for his rights."[9]

Under intense cross-examination, the prosecutor questioned Hines' proficiency and alleged mild demeanor.

> Moebes: "Did you tell Detective Ward that Tommy Hines exhibited animosity and became increasingly harder to take supervision from whites?"
>
> Dunlap: "Yes, I said that."
>
> Moebes: "Did you tell detective Ward that you thought he had picked this up from his family?"
>
> Dunlap: "I don't believe I said it that way, but I don't deny it."

---

[7] Ibid.
[8] Ibid.
[9] (Dunnavant, Rape Defense Loses Argument. Written Confession Allowed 1978)

Moebes: "Isn't it true that Tommy Hines would have been transferred from Cherry Street School to Calhoun Community College, for training, except for the objection of his parents?"

Dunlap: "No, I don't believe I said it that way."[10]

When Dunlap finished testifying, he returned to his seat in the courtroom.

Greg Owens, an attendance officer at the Developmental Center, communicated to the court that Tommy had only missed one day of school during the year. On the day of the attack school was out, he said.

A secretary at the Center, Rosemary Wright, testified, "He's a fine boy."[11] Often Tommy accompanied her during the three-mile drive, when she picked up the school's lunches from Brookhaven Middle School. Ms. Wright said that Hines had "always been well-mannered and polite at all times."[12]

Pat Gordon, bus driver and aide, spoke about Tommy's behavior as a student. She informed the court about his performance in homemaking courses, and skills in sanding and wood-staining classes. She stated that the defendant had never shown aggressive behavior.

Another witness, Allen Holmes revealed, "I could tell he was scared because his hands were shaking" (referring to when he visited Hines in jail).[13] Holmes was director of the Developmental Center and had been the only person permitted to see Tommy when he was first taken into custody.

Attorneys for the defense challenged Detective Ward's assertions that Hines was not under stress. The first witness to establish this claim was Jerry Cross, a trustee at the jail. Cross said that when he delivered lunch to Tommy Hines cell, the accused was "crying and praying."

Two black men, Floyd Jones and Eddie Marshall, who had been repairing carpet at city hall, were called to testify. Recalling the day the

---

[10] Ibid.
[11] (C. Wahl, Hines' Defense Could End Today 1978)
[12] (Burns, Rape Case May Go to Jurors By Weekend, Attorneys Predict 1978)
[13] Ibid.

defendant was arrested, both affirmed that Hines was not calm during the interrogation. Jones swore that around 2:30 or 3 p.m., he heard the defendant hollering, "Oh Lord, Leave me alone. Oh Lord, Oh Lord, my God, you leave me alone." Next, Marshall, who had peeped into the interrogation room when he and Jones had heard screaming, told jurors that Hines was sobbing. The defendant was saying, "Oh Lord Jesus, O Lord Jesus, I ain't done nothing."[14]

Neighbors and church members took the stand for a second time. All testified about Tommy's character, his kind demeanor, and mental incompetence to perform the crimes he had been charged with.

On Thursday afternoon, shortly after 3 p.m., Hines' co-counsels conferred with the judge. After about ten minutes, they returned to court and announced that they were dropping the insanity plea to "not guilty." Their strategy to plead "Not guilty by reason of insanity" had allowed them to get Hines' mental retardation diagnosis into the record. The defense rested.

In rebuttal, the state called two witnesses, Dr. Thomas Smith and Dr. Edwin Seger. A psychiatrist and attorney, Dr. Smith was the first to be called. He had examined the accused at Bryce pursuant to the June 23 ruling. A week earlier, in the absence of the jury, he had provided testimony. When questioned by the district attorney, Smith swore that Hines could understand his Miranda Rights, and could function sexually.

The ill feelings building in the room were extremely palpable. Hairston stood to cross. From the outset, the questioning was fierce. The pitch in his voice was a little louder and more forceful than was his usual manner. Hairston first pressed the doctor about his client's ability to understand his Miranda Rights. The doctor defended his reasoning.

Suddenly, the pressure intensified when the defense counsel asked Dr. Smith if he had examined the defendant's genitals.

"Yes, not by physical examination, but." Smith abruptly stopped speaking, interrupted by the defense attorney.

"That is what I mean, observe with your eyes, with your eyes, sir,

---

[14] (Hines v. State, 1980)

did you make a physical observation and examination of the defendant's genitalia?" Hairston insisted.

"I did in the courtroom," Smith retorted. "I saw that he had an erection one time."

"Objection!" bellowed Hairston.

"Overruled!" the judge shouted.

"You asked, I don't know," Dr. Smith snarled.

"I was asking during your examination," Hairston defended.

"You asked me about an examination," Smith responded.

"I asked you had you ever observed his genitalia during your examination," the lawyer countered.

After a volley of words between the expert witness and lawyer, Hairston shouted, "You knew [sic] what I asked you."[15]

Striking his gavel, Judge Riley dismissed the jury. In a stinging roar, he ordered the defense attorney to apologize. Riley stressed that no witness would be mistreated in his court. Hairston expressed regret. "I of course apologize for my somewhat improper response." In a defiant shift, he added that Dr. Smith's comments were "gratuitous, scandalous, and calculated to prejudice the jury."[16] The courtroom buzzed.

Calling the jury back in, the judge charged the twelve to disregard the last questions and answers, "erase [them] from your minds."

Next on the witness stand, Moebes called Dr. Edwin Seger, Chief of Psychology at Bryce Hospital in Tuscaloosa, Alabama. Seger had been a consultant on the team that decided Tommy Hines was fit to stand trial. Based on his professional opinion, he testified that the defendant was retarded. However, the psychologist determined that according to Hines' skills, he possessed a "mental age of 15 years and 5 months."[17] He told the court that when Tommy arrived at Bryce, he was afraid since it was the first time he'd been away from home and his parents. Seger stated that the defendant was "praying, calling his mother and father, crying and screaming, and had to be put in seclusion."[18] The

---

[15] (Hines v. State, 1980)
[16] (C. Wahl, Tommy Hines Case Expected to Reach Jury Today 1978)
[17] (Hines v. State, 1980)
[18] Ibid.

doctor concluded that Hines "could understand his constitutional rights if they were in plain words." He added, "In my opinion, if the rights on that sheet were just read to him, as you would read to a normal person, he would not be able to understand it. However, if they were explained."[19]

"I object to the latter part," Mims clamored.

"Overruled," hammered the judge.

Elaborating more extensively, Seger gave further details about Hines' ability to grasp his constitutional rights. "If they were explained to him, some of the words in there are large three syllable words, if they were broken down to where a person, a teenager could understand them, yes he could understand."[20]

Setting in motion a lengthy cross-examination, Hairston grilled the witness on the explanation of words in the Miranda that the defendant might or might not be able to comprehend:

> Hairston: "If you cannot afford a lawyer, one will be appointed for you if you wish, what about that one, sir?"
>
> Seger: "That would also have to be broken down."
>
> Hairston: "All right. What words would have to be explained and defined to the Defendant in order for him to understand that, sir?"
>
> Seger: "Afford, for one, I don't think he would know what the word afford would mean, if you can't pay, something like that. Also the word lawyer, when asked if he wanted to talk to the attorney, he knew what a lawyer was when I talked to him."
>
> Hairston: "How do you know that he understood?"
>
> Seger: "Well, we are getting back to what we talked about earlier."
>
> Hairston: "What did he say to you that indicated that he understood what a lawyer was?

---

[19] Ibid.
[20] Ibid.

Moebes: "Objection to that as being repetitious."

Judge Riley: "One more time, Mr. Moebes."

Seger: "When I was talking to him about a lawyer and the fact that when a lawyer came to see him and we told him that there was a lawyer out there to see you, one that was sent to Tuscaloosa by a black organization to see him, he knew that was the lawyer."[21]

After forceful prodding by the defendant's counsel, Dr. Seger finally conceded that "the stressful situation surrounding the defendant's being placed in and interrogated in police custody would inhibit his intellectual functioning to a degree."[22]

Taking a few steps forward, the interrogator asked if the accused was capable of assisting his attorneys with his defense. Seger answered, "I asked him hypothetical questions such as if your lawyer told you to plead guilty, would you do it, he said yes." "I asked him if he understood the charges and he asked what charges?"

"How did you know he was just saying yes?" question Hairston.

"From the way he looked, the way he sounded, the way he seemed to be following what I was saying," answered Seger.

"So when he says yes, he understood, but when he asked what charges, he's faking?" the defense asked.

"I'd say he's hedging," the doctor responded.[23]

Satisfied, he had weakened the case and discredited the mental health consultant, Hairston responded, "No further questions." He sat down. The witness was excused.

When Henry Mims, lead counsel for the plaintiff, stood for his closing summation, all eyes were on him. First, he thanked everyone, and then masterfully painted his picture.

"They classified Tommy Lee Hines with an IQ of 39," he said. "They said that he is at the moderate level of retardation, that he would be classed as trainable. But that didn't mean trained to fly an airplane

---

[21] Ibid.

[22] Ibid.

[23] (C. Wahl, Tommy Hines Case Expected to Reach Jury Today 1978)

or to command a submarine. That meant trained to cope with the rudiments of life – how to go to the bathroom, how to mop a floor."[24]

In an attempt to persuade the jurors of his client's innocence, Mims' further argued that there was no possibility that Hines could "conceive, plan and carry out such a rape." He reminded the twelve men and women, "The victim told this court that the rapist was rational. The state of Alabama would have you believe that on February 16 and that again on May 23 (the day Hines was arrested) that Tommy Lee Hines became rational."[25]

Attacking the evidence, Mims firmly declared that the ostensible confession signed by the defendant is "in perfect grammar, ordered from beginning to end."[26] He maintained that police forced Tommy to acknowledge guilt when he didn't understand. As he walked up to the evidence table, he pointed to the purported confessions. The lead counsel then moved closer to the jurors. He looked them in their eyes, and shockingly announced, "He signed the statements. He would have signed a hundred more if they had asked him to."[27] Submitting his hour-long closing argument, Mims sat down.

Next, Mike Moebes, Morgan County's district attorney, appealed to the court. Standing behind the respondent and his lawyers, he opened. "Tommy Hines 'functioned in the community as an individual. They didn't lead him around on a leash.'[28] The defense has been telling you that Tommy Lee Hines is the victim in this case, but the victim who suffered the wrong is not Tommy Lee Hines. He's not the victim of anything. How many nights do you think she cried and prayed since she was raped?'"[29]

Moebes went on, "Tommy Lee Hines has not been before you for two weeks because he is mentally retarded." Speaking louder, he exclaimed, "The defendant stands charged before you with raping

---

[24] (Cantrell, Tommy Hines gets 30 years 1978)
[25] Ibid.
[26] Ibid.
[27] Ibid.
[28] Ibid.
[29] Ibid.

this young lady." Directing attention to the victim, he pointed and bellowed, "She sits here for every female in society, for the rights of womanhood."[30] The prosecutor construed that based on the evidence provided, the signed confessions, and the victim's identification of her attacker; Hines was guilty. Moebes ended his summation.

Addressing the jurors, the judge explained the elements of reasonable doubt, guilty, and not guilty. As soon as they had been instructed on the law, the nine men and three women settled in for deliberation. It was 3:30 p.m. After a little over two and a half hours, the jury foreman advised the bailiff to let the judge know that a verdict had been rendered.

At the news that a decision had been made, people poured back into the courtroom. Hines' supporters filed in and sat behind him. The victim's family and a few friends sat behind her, including members of the Klan and white supremacists. Media filled the back seats. A large police presence collected to keep the peace. Emotions were high. Folks sat talking and waiting for the judge to come in.

When the magistrate walked in and sat down behind the large platform and the jury had taken their seats, he warned, "no outburst." As with all cases, the jurist asked, "Ladies and gentleman of the jury, have you reached a verdict?"

"We have your honor," the foreman said. "We the jury find the defendant, guilty."

There was complete silence. The judge told Tommy to stand and asked if he had anything to say to the court before pronouncing sentence.

Softly, Tommy whispered, "No sir."[31]

A thirty-year sentenced was pronounced. According to *The Tennessean*, the judge later admitted "it was the longest sentence for rape that he had handed down in his six year career."[32]

Mr. Richard Hines, Sr. was allowed a short visit with his son. Tommy was then cuffed and escorted by four carloads of state troopers to the

---

[30] (Cantrell, Tommy Hines gets 30 years 1978)
[31] (Dunnavant, 'Good Boy' Hines Gets 30 Years for Rape in Alabama 1978)
[32] Ibid.

Mount Meigs Correctional Center. Hines still faced three remaining charges, two of rape and a robbery.

It was Friday, October 13, 1978.

**March on Cullman, Alabama
October 1978**
Front: *L-R*. Larry Kirk, Morgan County SCLC chapter president, the Rev. John Nettles, Alabama SCLC president and marchers.

Courtesy: Alabama Department of Archives and History.
Donated by Alabama Media Group.
Photo by Tony Triolo, *Huntsville Times*.

L-R. The Rev. John Nettles and Dr. Joseph Lowery, National Southern Christian Leadership President, flanked by law enforcement at Cullman, Alabama.

Courtesy: Alabama Department of Archives and History.
Donated by Alabama Media Group.
Photo by Jones, *Birmingham News*.

Top. *L-R*: Dr. Joseph Lowery, Michael Guster, R. B. Cottonreader, Cullman Police Chief, Roy Wood (front)

Bottom. Police barrier separate Klansmen and white supremacists from SCLC and Black protestors.

Courtesy: Alabama Department of Archives and History. Donated by Alabama Media Group. Photos by Jones, *Birmingham News*.

Top. Sign holders at Cullman.
Bottom. *L-R*: J. Guster, John Anthony Rice, D. White

Courtesy: Alabama Department of Archives and History.
Donated by Alabama Media Group.
Photo by Jones, *Birmingham News*.

Top. Klansmen antagonize SCLC demonstrators
Bottom. SCLC Demonstrators blocked by law enforcement.

Images Courtesy: Alabama Department of Archives and History.
Donated by Alabama Media Group.
Photo by Jones, *Birmingham News*.

Verdict

Top. *L-R*: Clem "Doc" Peoples, UI, Cottonreader,
Mrs. Evelyn Lowery, and UI
Bottom. Unidentified woman carrying sign.

Images Courtesy: Alabama Department of Archives and History.
Donated by Alabama Media Group.
Photo by Tony Triolo, *Huntsville Times*.

Top. Mr. Richard Hines, Sr. *(suit)* and Hines Activists
Bottom. *L-R:* UI, Richard Hines, Sr., Hines,
Rice *(back)* Guster, Williams

Courtesy: Alabama Department of Archives and History.
Donated by Alabama Media Group.
Photo by Tony Triolo, *Huntsville Times*.

Verdict

Top. Tommy Lee Hines *(center)* going into Courthouse
Courtesy: Alabama Department of Archives and History.
Donated by Alabama Media Group.
Photo by Jones, *Birmingham News*.

Bottom. Arrest being made
Courtesy: Alabama Department of Archives and History.
Donated by Alabama Media Group.
Photo by Tony Triolo, *Huntsville Times*.

CHAPTER 12

What Lies Ahead

Returning home to Decatur, members of the local SCLC considered the events of the Tommy Hines saga, particularly, the last two weeks of the trial. They discussed plans to appeal the thirty-year conviction and plotted strategies for the up-coming cases.

On October 23, a mass meeting was held at First Baptist, on Vine Street. In a crowded house, John Nettles, SCLC's national vice president, addressed the crowd before introducing Dr. Joseph Lowery, the national president. Promising the organization's continued support, and his own, Nettles assured them, "We're going to kneel-in, pray in, stand in, and do whatever kind of 'in' it takes to free Tommy Hines."[1] The assembly agreed with thunderous applause and amens.

Dr. Lowery rose. Speaking distinctly, he praised Hines' supporters for their commitment and peaceful actions during the last five months. He then encouraged everyone to get involved in the movement to get Hines released, particularly his fellow clergymen. His passionate preacher's voice roared, "You are never going to have the kind of movement you need here in Decatur until you get your preachers involved. Our movement is a religious movement[;] We never want God to be on the outside."[2]

Castigating Morgan County district attorney's depiction of Hines, Lowery explained Moebes efforts to brand the mentally disabled defendant. "Tommy Hines is a militant black man who was mad at whites – so he went around raping white women."[3] The preacher

---

[1] (Field, Broader Support Asked for Hines 1978)
[2] Ibid.
[3] Ibid.

proclaimed, "Tommy Hines is still an innocent young man. You see, in order to acquit Tommy Hines, it would be saying that the justice system in Decatur, Morgan and Cullman counties is a rotten, racist system." He reckoned, "It's pitiful. It's Tommy Lee Hines who has been raped by justice." Lowery said, "If this nation is going to be saved, God is going to do it through blacks."[4]

At the prompting of Dr. Joseph Lowery, the family was persuaded to engage the services of Birmingham lawyer and state representative, Uriah "U. W." Clemon, to represent their son. Howard Moore, an attorney who represented activists Angela Davis and Julian Bond, was asked to assist him. Clemon had been SCLC's civil rights attorney, and Moore had successfully worked with the NAACP Legal Defense Fund. A strife brewed between the former defense team and the new legal representatives.

Born in Fairfield, Alabama, U. W. Clemon received his undergraduate degree from Miles College, and because he wasn't allowed to attend the University of Alabama's law school, the state of Alabama paid for him to attend Columbia University in New York. Earning his law degree in 1968, he returned home and was among the first ten blacks to be admitted to the Alabama bar. Clemon was a well-known civil rights attorney.[5] Familiar to some blacks in North Alabama, he had handled many of the desegregation cases. The lawyer was famously known for successfully suing Paul "Bear" Bryant to integrate the University of Alabama's football team. He also waged war with Governor George Wallace to include blacks on state boards. Adding to his list of accomplishments, in 1974 he was one of two state senators elected to the Alabama Senate since Reconstruction. Appointed by President Jimmy Carter, U. W. Clemon became Alabama's first African American to serve as a federal judge. From 1999-2006, he was Chief Judge of the United States District Court for the Northern District of Alabama.[6]

Both attorneys, Mims and Clemon, filed appeals. Both claimed to

---

[4] Ibid.
[5] (Clemon 2001)
[6] (Wikipedia 2019)

be the attorney of record. In mid-November, Mims filed a 16-count motion on behalf of his Tommy Hines in the Cullman Circuit Court. Included was a motion for a new trial and a motion for reduced sentence, which would allow bond while Hines waited for the appeal. Mims expressed, "I have a legal obligation to represent Hines. To give up this case now would be contrary to everything I've done for months to help this kid."[7]

Clemon filed a notice for appearance and a motion for a new trial, stating that Mr. Hines' parents had discharged Mims who had a "professional responsibility to withdraw from the case." In discussing the trial, the civil rights lawyer noted, "There were certain issues in our judgement that were not raised effectively."[8] He cited retraction of the "not guilty by reason of insanity plea, an improvident withdrawal."[9] Judge Riley designated the Birmingham lawyer as the lead counsel and Mims as second lead. Clemon's would later say, the two "worked together for the benefit of [the] welfare of Tommy Lee Hines."[10]

Meanwhile Cullman County sent Morgan County a bill in the amount of $4,621.72 to abet trial expenses.

On Friday, Dec. 15, Brother Manuel Whitfield, an African American minister from Columbus, Georgia, arrived at Cullman, Alabama. Disquieting many of its town citizens, he used the courthouse steps as his pulpit. Beginning his impromptu sermon, he read scripture and shook his Bible frantically at his hearers. Exhorting fairness, he cried out, "Tommy Lee Hines is one of God's children."[11] His voice, full of fervor, rose to a high pitch as he condemned the Oct. 13 sentencing. A crowd of white people gathered to see the unwanted preacher. Some stayed for the duration of the sermon. Others hung around for a while and then moved on. Delivering this message to his congregants was no easy task. Entrenched in racism, many of the observers loudly sang

---

[7] (Cantrell, Hines Case Attorneys Squabbling 1978)
[8] Ibid.
[9] Ibid.
[10] (Cantrell, Hines Lawyer Agree To Join Forces 1979)
[11] (Federal Authorities Checking Beating of Black Man Locally 1978)

choruses of racial insults and racial epithets. Finally, after about three hours, Whitfield ended his fiery sermon.

Leaving Cullman, Whitfield was abducted. An FBI agent investigating the incident said that three white men bolted out of a black van and dragged Whitfield about a mile into the woods. They stripped and beat him with tree limbs. A passing motorist witnessed the man being carried off and called Cullman police.[12] After searching the area, police found the preacher and rushed him to the hospital. Whitfield was treated for injuries to his head and back. "Maybe he will think twice before returning to Cullman," Bill McGlocklin said, admitting that the Ku Klux Klan was responsible for the attack.[13] McGlocklin was grand klaliff, second in command of the Alabama Klan organization. He operated a service station on 6th Avenue in Decatur, Alabama.

"It's like a dog – if you got a dog or a horse you can't tame, every once in a while you just have to take a switch to them," McGlocklin declared. Later, he did acknowledge that the white supremacist group participated in the abduction but not the whipping. A week later, recanting his remarks, the grand klaliff said, "I was given the wrong information. But if it was our men, we stand behind them 100%. That man is a raving maniac."[14]

Refusing to press charges, Brother Whitfield said the Klan were God's children too, and "It isn't the Christian thing to do."[15] The Federal justice department was ordered to investigate.

To protest injustice and the abduction and beating of Brother Manuel Whitfield, on December 22, a carload of ministers from Decatur journeyed to Cullman to preach on the courthouse steps. Among them were preachers, R. B. Cottonreader, Clem "Doc" Peoples, Arthur Turner of Nazarene Missionary Baptist Church at Barton, and Tim Harris, pastor of Courtland Primitive Baptist Church, in Courtland, and Manuel Whitfield. They preached and prayed and in the midst of the mini-sermons, over forty plus whites started singing "Dixie"

---

[12] (Klan Leader Admits Attack on Black Minister 1978)
[13] (Klan admits Black's Abduction 1978)
[14] (Dunnavant, Cullman State Set for Klan, Black Faceoff 1978)
[15] Ibid.

and yelling "White Power." Blacks responded by singing "We Shall Overcome." Doc Peoples, a combat veteran, told the congregating whites that "blacks were not afraid of their enemies."[16] Mission accomplished, the blacks returned to the Decatur's SCLC headquarters.

The following month, during a Federal Court hearing, McGlocklin testified that he had no knowledge of Whitfield's kidnapping and beating. He swore that his previous "statements were based on inaccurate information."[17]

On a cold day in mid-February, 1979, a clash between SCLC members and the Klan occurred in the parking lot of the A&P Supermarket, in Decatur's Westgate Shopping Center. A black man had been taken into custody on the evening of Tuesday, Feb. 6, and charged with shop lifting. Tommy Lee Hines' 30 year conviction, and upcoming trials; coupled with racial contentions; were like smoldering embers. This occurrence only contributed to fanning the flame. Believing the arrest was harassment, coupled with other grievances against the only neighborhood grocery store in the West Town area, SCLC led a protest. A&P's customers were primarily Blacks. There were no people of color employed as cashiers, and the community shoppers complained about receiving rotting meat as well. Standing across the front entrance of the supermarket African Americans picketed the store on Friday and Saturday. On Saturday, the market closed early.

That Sunday morning about 30 blacks and 65 whites met in the parking lot on Moulton Street. Wielding guns, both sides attempted to intimidate the other. State troopers in riot gear positioned themselves between the angry blacks and whites. Fortunately, there was no violence. Cottonreader maintained that the SCLC has a non-violence philosophy and that those in the group with guns were there to possibly protect the demonstrators. As Ronald Williams was leaving, a shotgun riddled the back side of his car.[18] Cottonreader and Charles Bowman were arrested for "unlawful assembly and conspiracy to interfere with a business."

---

[16] (Cullman Scene of Demonstration 1978)
[17] (Times 1979)
[18] (Protestors Are Given Trial Date 1979)

On Feb.19, 1979, after the counterdemonstration at the A&P, a city ordinance prohibiting guns during a demonstration was passed.

The Cullman City Council, on March 2, 1979, declined to issue parade permits to both the Ku Klux Klan and SCLC members.

At a March 12 Decatur city council meeting, hooded and robed Klan packed the room, opposing the recent gun ordinance, and citing it as "gestapo tactics." A verbal face-off caused rising tension between the racist group, Cottonreader, and the interracial council. The SCLC leader had vowed to disrupt every meeting if a Klan was added to the panel. Claiming victory, no known Klan was placed on the board.

Livid about the order, that Saturday a motorcade of robed Klansmen slowly maneuvered their way through Decatur streets. Packing the back of pickup trucks, members of the hate group stood with fists up, and yelled loudly, "White Power." They waved weapons, guns, lead pipes, sticks, and American and Confederate flags. Passing by Mayor Duke's house, one of the leaders yelled out, "If the mayor wants our guns, he'll have to come after them."[19] Denying that the ordinance violated the constitutional rights to "bear arms," Bill Dukes said it was to protect lives. "What price do you place on human life," he pronounced.

A hearing was held to consider a change of venue for the other two rape and robbery trials. Psychological testing that had been conducted established Hines mental age at 4.6 years, rather than 6.4 years as previously proven. Reporters from various media outlets were called upon to testify about the trial publicity. A mound of newspaper articles and newsreels from all over the United States were presented to Judge Riley, to support the fact that it was impossible for the defendant to receive a fair trial in Cullman. After much consideration, Judge Riley granted the motion for a change of venue from Cullman to Birmingham. Setting precedence, it was the first time in the state's history that a defendant had been granted a second change of venue. Alabama law cited only one change of venue per trial.[20] Riley contended that racial tension made it impossible for Hines to receive a fair trial

---

[19] (AP, KKK Members Defy Weapons Ban 1979)
[20] (Judge Moves Rape Trial of Hines to Birmingham 1979)

in Cullman. He ruled that the "state statute [was] superseded by the Sixth Amendment to the Constitution, which guarantees trial by an impartial jury, and the 14th Amendment, which provides for due process of law."[21] Immediately, Mike Moebes contacted the State Attorney General, Charlie Graddick, to petition the Alabama Court of Criminal Appeals to overturn Judge Riley's decision.

Henry Mims withdrew from the case.

When the Appellate Court upheld Riley's decision to transfer the trial to Jefferson County, Graddick requested the state Supreme Court to intervene. The high court refused.

---

[21] Ibid.

CHAPTER 13

Looming Danger

"We shall overcome, We shall overcome, We shall overcome, some day," the protestors sang. Ooooh, deep in my heart, I do believe, We shall overcome, some day."

Singing the familiar civil rights anthem, an exuberant crowd of about seventy, led by Dr. Lowery, left the Wayman Chapel AME Church.[1] It was Saturday, May 26, 1979. The Memorial Day weekend march was in observance of the one year anniversary of Tommy Hines arrest. Doc Peoples was out front with his dog, "Husky." Demonstrators were together mostly in twos or threes. Rev. Lowery's wife, Evelyn, followed the marchers in the family's 1977 Buick, along with other private vehicles.

Caught up in the euphoria of the moment, the jubilant group marched along Bank Street, in route to City Hall. They loudly repeated their chants. Before leaving the church, the protestors had reflected on Friday's Alabama Supreme Court ruling that upheld a second change of venue to Birmingham, not to mention, that U. W. Clemon would represent Hines in the upcoming trials. Such triumphant victories were cause to make a joyful noise.

Hearing that both the Ku Klux Klan and the SCLC were gathering to march, the Police and Sheriff's Department had called in extra manpower.

Klansmen and other white supremacists had assembled near

---

[1] Wayman Chapel African Methodist Episcopal (AME) church history can be traced as far back as 1877 when the Reverend T. W. Coffee was assigned to the Decatur Mission. The mission had six members. He served them six months, and received $12 for his services. (Seeking4 Truth)

the Purina Warehouse loading dock close to Lee and Davis Streets. The turn-out included men in white robes and hoods, and others in street clothes, including women and children. Some of them stood near parked cars and trucks with doors stretched wide open. About a hundred Klansmen stood in the middle of the street. Lingering casually, they armed themselves with big sticks, axe handles, and batons. Chants of "White Power" and "Unfair Treatment" echoed loudly. Ferocious Dobermans and German Shepherds snarled and barked. Secured to a homemade gallows, in the back of one of the pickup trucks was a stuffed dummy that dangled with a noose around its neck. A hand-written note on the effigy read "Tommy Hines."[2]

Proceeding down Bank Street, the demonstrators' singing, clapping and chanting, grew louder and louder. Near the front of the procession, a station wagon slowly meandered its way through the street. A medium-height man walked beside the rear of the car. As blacks approached the curve where the thoroughfare turns into Lee Street, they could not see what waited ahead. A sea of whites moved in tightly to block the way. Police Chief Pack Self radioed for officers to take action and remove the Klan so that the blacks could pass. Despite police orders to move, Ray Steele, a regional Klan officer, ordered his group to hold their position.

Then, Steele led them in a vociferous chant, bellowing, "What do we want?"

"White power!" His comrades screamed.[3]

Peace officers in riot gear sandwiched themselves between the opposing groups, in an effort to disperse the Klan. Like thunder, hateful cursing and enraged belligerent rants clattered through the air.

Getting closer, the demonstrators could see the street filled with men in white robes, who attempted to block the parade. Reverend R. B. Cottonreader lifted his bullhorn and shouted into it, "Please clear the street. We're not stopping – we're coming through!"[4] A second time, he roared, "We are not stopping, so clear the street." The protestors

---

[2] (Sherill 1979)
[3] (King 1979)
[4] Ibid.

continued walking. They sang even louder, "Ain't gonna let nobody turn me around, turn me around, turn me around. Ain't gonna let nobody turn me around." Regardless of the angry white crowd, they advanced, working their way closer.

Meeting their gaze, enraged voices bellowed from the opposite side, "Niggers, that's as far as you go. Niggers, go home. You niggers will not march here. You'll never march here again!" Other's raucously agreed.

Swinging axe handles, clubs, and tree limbs, Klansmen forced their way through the police line. Blacks strained to get past the human barrier. Doc Peoples weaved his way around with his leashed dog. Several of the whites grabbed him. Police seized one of the men, a number of his white buddies yelled, "Let him go now."[5] Within that same moment, other front line blacks forced their way through the blockade.

Bashed heads and body parts thudded underneath clubs and fist, as the opposing groups came to blows. Some of the Klansmen rushed to their vehicles. One of them lurched forward, and swung a large red axe handle, back and forth at a police officer. A couple of the cops ran in and rushed the man down.

Suddenly, there was a loud cry. "He's got a gun. He's got a gun. He's got a gun in his pocket," a man said, pointing to a male who had been walking beside the rear of a station wagon. "Why don't they arrest him?" one of the white men demanded.[6] Police and Klan ran toward the brown-skinned, medium-framed man.

Bang. Bang. Bang.

"They're shooting! They're shooting!" some of the blacks shouted hysterically. More than 20 sporadic gun shots rang out within a minute. Panic-stricken people scattered. Running for their lives, they rolled under cars, hid on the sides of buildings, and ducked inside cars that were holding the rear. Many of the women and children screamed; some fell to the ground as others bolted back down Bank Street. Whites

---

[5] Ibid.
[6] (Sherill 1979)

chased after them, swinging their clubs and cursing. Amid the mayhem, Dr. Lowery was rushed away by his aides.

David Kelso, president of the local Klan group, cried out, "Help me boys, I'm shot."[7] As the man collapsed onto the pavement, a few of his friends ran to his aid. As they pulled back his white robe, crimson blood oozed from his chest and colored his shirt. Applying pressure on the wound, one of them screamed, "Call an ambulance!"

"Fall back! Fall back!" A command was given. One of the leaders of the Klansmen shouted, "Stop boys. Hold it!"[8] They withdrew.

Many of the counter-demonstrators scurried into parked vehicles and ran toward the courthouse for safety. A man standing in the back of his truck cocked his gun, and fired shots toward the retreating marchers. Seeing defenseless women and children under attack, a couple of men among the blacks started firing as well. Bullets flew from every direction – the Klan, the blacks and police all were shooting.

To escape the chaos, cars accelerated and skidded onto side streets, while others made U-turns onto the sidewalks and sped away.

In the fracas, a tall, slender, mahogany-skinned woman felt a piercing pain. A warm fluid flowed down her cheek. Bernice Brown had been shot in the face. Larry Smith held his left temple after suffering a gunshot wound, and James "Spider" Chairs received injuries to the head. Along with Kelso, another white male, Berdice Kilgo bore a gunshot wound to his right leg.

With Lowery's car as a target, two bullets ripped into the vehicle. Mrs. Lowery ducked and stretched her body across the front seat. Shards of glass from the shattered windshield sprinkled her body. A round lodged into the dashboard and one struck the window frame. "Kill em all!"[9] she heard someone say while she took cover.

Dozens of police ran in every direction of the fired shots. Seeing Timothy Guster, one of the demonstrators, officers swarmed him. After witnessing women and children being fired upon, Guster immediately

---

[7] (Dunnavant, Klan Attacks Marchers. Gunfire Marks Decatur Battle 1979)
[8] Ibid.
[9] (Suggs 2013)

took action to shield them, until they could get away.[10] With guns pointed at his head, they pinned him down and pressed him against the Brock & Spight Wholesale building, on Bank Street. His older brother, James, ran over and cautioned him, "Don't move man. Don't move." Warning police, the elder brother urged, "You all don't want to hurt anyone." They cuffed the suspect and put him into a police car that was parked near where the Klan had clustered. Several minutes passed before he was taken to jail and charged with disorderly conduct.

"Stop! Stop now or we will shoot!" an officer shouted, hoisting his gun in pursuit of John Rice. The black man abruptly ended his run. Several police and sheriff deputies shoved him down. While Rice was lying prostrate on the ground, a policeman charged, "Put your hands behind your head, now!" They pointed their guns at him. Picking Rice up, officers led him away in handcuffs, pushed him into a squad car, and carried him to jail.

Minutes afterward, an officer forcibly grabbed Deran Godfrey by the arm and handcuffed him. Arrested for disorderly conduct, he was taken to city hall.

After the shooting, the stuffed dummy was pulled off its stand, thrown in the street, beaten and burned by the Klan.[11]

Before the march began, a few of the blacks had armed themselves in fear of a white mob attack. James Guster, James Chairs, and John Anthony Rice, had been on a scouting expedition earlier that morning. They observed a sea of flowing white robes at a KKK meeting in a park, just across the Tennessee River Bridge, on Highway 31. The Klan openly girded themselves with rifles, pistols, ax handles and the like. Returning to the church, where Hines supporters prepared for the march, the three recounted what they had seen.[12] The sheriff had also notified SCLC members that the Klan was not going to let them march. Additionally, Cottonreader had informed Dr. Lowery about information overheard on a Klansman's CB radio. The message was "Get Lowery

---

[10] (T. Guster 2020)
[11] (Sherill 1979)
[12] (Guster 2019)

and Nettles" and others.[13] After much discussion about the potential threat of violence, they prayed and decided that their only option was to march. Upholding SCLC's nonviolence concepts, Lowery had reminded Hines' demonstrators of the organization's peaceful approach and that they were Christians.

Frantic and breathing hard, individuals finally made their way back to the safety of the AME church, with only minor scrapes. Other than the three that had been rushed to the hospital, and those arrested, all were accounted for. No casualties. Visibly shaken, Mrs. Lowery, found her way back to the sanctuary. She had a few cuts from the scattered glass. Nothing life threatening.

In seeking to make sense of what had just happened, Dr. Lowery stood up and spoke. First, he endeavored to calm the group. Then, he rallied forcefully: "What you have witnessed here today is a complete breakdown of law and order. The Ku Klux Klan will not put fear in our hearts. They will put faith in our hearts. God will roll back the KKK, and He will roll back the racist attitudes of the state of Alabama."[14]

Meanwhile, the hostile faction gathered to review the day's events. Ray Steele, a regional Klan officer, stood on the back of his truck, and vowed, "We will retaliate. I guarantee you, we will come back. If I have to stand by myself, they (blacks) will not march again in Decatur, Alabama. And we will never get caught without our weapons again."[15]

"Decatur will regret the day this happened. Some Blacks marched up here with guns but the police made us put ours away. We left our guns in our cars but we've taken them out now!" somebody else yelled.

Bill Wilkinson said in a statement, "I don't see how our men can oppose the niggers in Decatur unarmed again. It's better than being killed and obviously the police in Decatur are not protecting our people. I don't see how we can be asked to stand by while the Negroes carry guns,"[16]

---

[13] (Lowery 2011)

[14] (Dunnavant, Klan Attacks Marchers. Gunfire Marks Decatur Battle 1979)

[15] (Hayes, Wahl and Wayne, More Arrests Possible in Race Melee As Police Probe Shootings of 4 Here 1979)

[16] Ibid.

Retribution was swift. That Saturday night, two white-owned stores in the Old Town Community were shot up and another was looted. Two others were torched; the Busy Bee Market received heavy damage, and Tip Top Foods suffered minor property damage. While firefighters attempted to extinguish the fires, sniper bullets were fired at police, who had surrounded the stores. Donny Garth was arrested and while being handcuffed, more shots were fired. Garth's .22 caliber loaded rifle was confiscated.[17] During a search of a nearby alley, more weapons were found. The owners had fled. Several law enforcement agencies continued to monitor the river town throughout the weekend.

At a Black Caucus meeting in Birmingham that same evening, Dr. Lowery described his near death experience, only a few hours earlier. While speaking, he urged Caucus members to join him in the next march. Lowery asked Congressman John Conyers (Detroit) to contact the Federal Justice Department.[18] That Sunday, United States Attorney General, Griffin Bell, (President Carter's Administration) assured Conyers of an investigation. Monday morning Decatur buzzed with agents from the Federal Bureau of Investigation (FBI).

On Monday, authorities arrested Curtis Robinson (Red Goose) a city Maintenance Department worker. It had widely been reported that Robinson was the man who shot Kelso. He was charged with intent to murder.[19]

Reaching a boiling point, the year-long simmering contention had exploded. This was the first time that violence had occurred. It was never clear where the first shot came from. Both sides blamed the other, and some said the first shots were from police.

Both Mayor Dukes and Governor Fob James called the madness that had erupted deplorable. James promised that he would do everything in his power to ensure peaceful demonstrators would be protected.

Counterdemonstrations were planned for June 9.

---

[17] (FBI Sent to Decatur After Saturday Racial Shootings 1979)
[18] Ibid.
[19] (Hayes and Field, Klansman Shooting Charged to Man 1979)

CHAPTER 14

Not an Ordinary Parade

June 9, 1979, was no ordinary spring day. They came in packs from every southern state and several northern ones as well. Thousands of civil rights protestors and Hines' advocates disembarked from buses, vans, and automobiles at the Carrie Matthews Recreation Center. Across town, every street and alley adjacent to the Wayman Chapel AME Church at 412 Church Street was congested as demonstrators poured into the streets.

In a front yard on Church Street, three little girls laughed, tossed a ball, and ran joyfully as they played. Along the sidewalk, three bicycles were intentionally lined up, side by side, as if they were cars in a parking lot. Other toys were strewed around the yard and onto a grassy medium bordering the sidewalk. Dressed in the same style outfits, just different colors, the trio looked to be about eight or nine years old. Two of the girls, Petrina, who was tall and slender, and Cynthia, who was shorter, and a bit fuller, shared similar features. Their burnt sienna-brown skin was beautiful. They could have been twins. The other girl, Latrisha, was slightly taller, thin and with olive skin. Their hair was parted down the middle and pulled into two ponytails adorned with matching colorful rope ribbons.

An overwhelming excitement overtook the trio as they watched a parade of people flood their neighborhood. The older woman explained the reasons for the invasion. "They're marching for Tommy Lee Hines, a retarded boy who was arrested for something he didn't do," she said. "They're marching for our rights."

The meaning of the march was far beyond their comprehension, yet they begged to go on this pilgrimage, "Mama, please, please, let us go." She answered with a booming, "No." No further explanation was needed; it was Momma.

The plump lady's skin was a soft shade of light caramel, and her brown eyes were kind. Her shoulder-length hair was bluish-gray and pulled back in a thick ponytail. She wore a short-sleeved blue dress. Keeping an attentive eye on the girls, her daughters and granddaughter, she marveled at the hundreds of people who took possession of her street. The mass of folk tried to congregate at or near the small AME church.

A strange man, tall and lean, brown-skinned tone, and wearing dark dress trousers and a white shirt, maneuvered his way toward the girls and the big white house, trimmed in green. He had a white hand towel flung over one shoulder.

The front yard was partially fenced with a lush green hedge row. Leading to the high porch on each side of the concrete steps were wing walls (most Southerners refer to them as a stoop) that extended out and doubled for both sitting and flower pots. A red-tinted front porch stretched the entire length of the house, bedecked with green and white porch furniture.

Stepping up onto the sidewalk leading to the house, he moved closer to the steps. Smiling, he spoke and introduced himself to the lady who was rocking back and forward gently on the front porch swing. Before he could say another word, the Allen matriarch sat up and asked, "Can I help you?"

"Hell-o ma'am," he said, "We are here because of racial injustices in Decatur, particularly the Tommy Hines case and the recent events that happened here." After some talk about the march, the minister turned to the woman and politely asked, "Ma'am, would you and your children join us? This is a historic moment."

The lady's face creased with a friendly smile. Not able to march because of a recent illness, the woman told the stranger that she was very familiar with all the events that had taken place in her home town. She expressed her feelings about the violence, even shootings. At that moment, fear grabbed her inner being. Her face and words exposed her concern. "I'm scared they will be hurt," she answered, referring to her daughters and granddaughter. After some discussion, and a promise to take care of the girls, the minister finally convinced the mother to allow the girls to join the rally.

Momentum was high. The crowd's enthusiasm rallied onlookers; some spontaneously left their yards to join the protesters. An unsettling calm shrouded the crowd. Pent up anger and emotions had intensified with the colossal cross burnings and growing presence of robed Ku Klux Klan. Raging emotions incinerated more with the latest stint of disturbances just two weeks earlier at the one-year anniversary march of Tommy Lee Hines' arrest. Some folk had worried that there might be more violence.

An enormous crowd estimated at more than 1,500 flooded the streets singing freedom songs. Many of the demonstrators carried "Free Tommy Hines" banners and homemade signs that read: "Justice"; "Ban the Klan"; "Decatur Justice is Retarded"; "God is on our Side"; and "Justice Now for Tommy Hines." Over and over, the demonstrators' clapped and shouted, "We're fired up!" "We're fired up!" We're fired up!" Chanting at the top of their voices, their cries grew louder. "We're fired up!" "We're fired up!" We're fired up!"

Briefly interrupting the chants, occasional instructions amplified by a bullhorn gave additional details. Sometime after, a prayer was offered. The group finally moved out. Although the crowd was so thick that the protestors could barely move, their determination and enthusiasm were not to be hindered.

The mass of people could be heard for blocks away: "Free Tommy Lee!" "Free Tommy Lee!" "Free Tommy Lee!"

Leading the grand parade were men carrying massive flags. The panoply of colors included the American flag; the red, black and green Afro American flag; the Southern Christian Leadership flag; and an oversized "Free Tommy Hines" banner that had his picture embossed in the middle. Marchers, both black and white, filled the street, line after line, and paraded slowly down Church Street from the historic Old Town Community, moving across the railroad tracks on Vine, toward Bank Street. Suddenly, one of the little girls felt a sting, then the trickle of something warm was felt in her tiny sandal. She cried out in pain as her two companions, who clutched her hands tightly, stopped to see what the matter was. Looking down, a cherry red fluid seeped out the side of her shoe. Closer inspection from an adult revealed that sharp tacks had been strewn in the street, and several went through the child's sandal, piercing her little foot. This was their first encounter with racism and their first involvement with a civil rights movement. Not to be deterred, they marched on.

Outraged and demanding justice, the massive movement was led by (SCLC) stalwarts, the Reverend Dr. Joseph Lowery, president; Reverends John Nettles, vice president; acting SCLC Executive Director, Fred Shuttlesworth; Ralph Abernathy, past president; and Bernard Lee. The night before, Rev. Lee had spoken at Wayman Chapel. A personal assistant to Dr. Martin Luther King, Jr., his message of justice for Tommy and the importance of nonviolence resonated.[1] The Rev. R. B. Cottonreader, field director, and Larry Kirk, local SCLC chapter president, were among them. Other notables included: civil rights activist the Rev. Cordy Tindell "C. T." Vivian, who often marched and planned events with the late Dr. Martin Luther King, Jr.; Tuskegee Mayor Johnny Ford; students and faculty from Notre Dame University; and the members of the Revolutionary Communist Party. Alvin Holmes and representatives from the Alabama Black Caucus, and members from State and Congressional Black Caucuses, including Walter Fauntroy, George "Mickey" Leland (Democrat-Texas), and the Georgia Legislature. Participants from the National Association for Advancement of Colored People (NAACP) chapters; African People's Socialist Party and the Charlotte Equal Rights Council were present.[2] Others who joined in the march were union members of various labor groups.

Law enforcement numbered about 400 strong. They included city and neighboring police and sheriff's departments, guardsmen with two armored personnel carriers, state troopers, agents from the State Alcoholic Beverage Control board, and the FBI. Most of them wore

---

[1] (Turner 1979)
[2] (Field, Hundreds Came to Join Tommy Hines March 1979)

riot gear and carried automatic weapons. Tear gas masks were hooked onto their belts.[3] Special agents had positioned themselves on rooftops of City Hall, the Courthouse, McRae Motors and other downtown buildings. Scanning the assembly, they kept a watchful eye on the swarm of people.[4] Helicopter blades vibrated from above.

Passing the location where the Blacks and Klansmen had clashed two weeks earlier, the massive crowd moved fearlessly onward. Reaching the Decatur Municipal building steps, Dr. Joseph Lowery looked all around him. Packed shoulder to shoulder, folk were crammed together. Throngs of individuals were near the rear of where he was standing, others in front and on both sides of him. As far as the eye could see, there were people and they were still coming. Some found refuge from the blistering heat under a small shade tree or umbrella. Tolerating the heat, most in the crowd fanned themselves with wooden-handled funeral home fans. Others used pamphlets or newspapers that had been handed out earlier. Certain ones had brought towels to wipe the sweat from their faces and necks. Frequently, they would flap the towel vivaciously from shoulder to shoulder for a light breeze.

About 200 robed Klansmen and white sympathizers assembled across the street shouting "White power!" "Dixie" played on a loudspeaker. Not to be drowned out, the throng of Blacks sang and chanted even louder.

All waited eagerly to hear Dr. Lowery speak.

A firecracker boomed near a construction trailer. The explosive noise caused many to jump.

The heat was intense in every way. Dr. Lowery begin. "Let me tell you how innocent Decatur is."

"Tell us!" the crowd shouted with enthusiasm, bodies perspiring as they stood in scorching hot sun.

"Let's set the record straight about Decatur. Decatur says the Klan and SCLC are using Decatur. They're saying Decatur is innocent.

---

[3] (Foreman 1979)
[4] Ibid.

Decatur is as innocent as Judas and as guilty as John Dillinger!" Lowery said.

"Amen," the protestors agreed.

"Decatur took a man with a child's mind, read him rights he couldn't understand."

"Tell it!" yelled the audience.

"Tried him in a county with no black jurors and put him in prison for 30 years for a crime he could not have committed. The hell with you, Decatur!"

"Amen!" The crowd cheered loudly.

"No, you're not innocent, Decatur. The Klan does not exist in a vacuum," Lowery preached. "They're able to exist because the so-called good people of Decatur refuse to speak out.

"The Chamber never advertised Decatur as the hometown of Tommy Hines. But that's how it became known. Not for Lurleen B. Wallace Developmental Center or for the world's first swimming pool [America's first wave pool], those are there too. But [the] Hines' case brought the civil rights marchers with T-shirts that said, 'Free Tommy Lee, God's Child'...Then the bullets. And the headlines and the TV news spots."[5]

"Black folks in this town have no say so in their law enforcement. Decatur has one black policeman, and they won't let him walk downtown."

"Discover Black people. We've come here to Decatur to declare that although we helped to discover America, much of America hasn't discovered us. Discover us, America! Our brains helped to defend America."[6] Lowery went on for thirty or more minutes.

Charged with excitement, the crowd resounded with ear-cracking cheers and thunderous applause.

Rev. R. B. Cottonreader stepped forward and reassured the assembly, "Although it's been said that this is the last march, this is just

---

[5] (Dart, Father, Tommy Lee Belongs Right Here 1980)
[6] (Field, Hundreds Came to Join Tommy Hines March 1979)

the beginning. We want the world to know that Tommy Lee Hines is innocent."[7] The mass of people cheered in jubilation.

Speaking on behalf of Washington DC's Black Caucus, civil rights activist and U.S. Representative Walter Fauntroy commended those gathered. "We've come here to say thank you courageous blacks of Decatur for standing up for freedom." "We've come here today to say to the Klan that we have the right to assemble peacefully and petition the government."[8]

Johnny Ford, Tuskegee mayor, told the group that "mayors all over the state have the responsibility to allow peaceful demonstrations. I wish some Ku Klux Klansmen would come to my town!"[9]

Earlier that morning, Klan demonstrators and white supremacy factions had met across the river at the park, waiting for their designated parade time, from 10 a.m. to noon. About 9:30, they began lining up at the corners of Lee and Bank Streets near the Valley Feed Company. Parading from the juncture where the shootings had occurred weeks earlier, they, too, walked to City Hall. The grand chaplain invoked God to grant "superiority over race-mixers, communists and liberals." He prayed, "As long as there is a white person in one of these robes in America, we will stand and not be moved…The more they oppress us, the more our ranks grow."

Other speakers attacked school integration and affirmative action. An 83 year-old minister preached, "They're black because Almighty God made them that way. God made blacks and called them to be servants, and He said (blacks) shall be that way all of their days."

Bill Wilkinson, the imperial wizard, told the crowd, "I'm sick of Negroes being given jobs that I deserve." Receiving booming applause, he went on to criticize local officials, saying they were more concerned about blacks than the whites.[10]

When all the speakers at the Hines demonstration finished, there

---

[7] Ibid.
[8] Ibid.
[9] Ibid.
[10] (Hayes 1979)

was hand clapping and cheers. The activists returned to the Wayman Chapel Church. The march ended with no violence.

Excited and exhausted by the day's events, the little girls told the Allen matriarch all about their adventure, as she cared for her daughter's injury. It was the girls' first exposure to a civil rights moment, and one that they'd never forget.

On Saturday, August 26, 1979, Klansmen led by their Imperial Wizard, Bill Wilkinson, and other anti-black participants, met in an empty lot on Lenwood Drive. Glass popped as a yellow school bus burned. Torched by children (members of the Klan Youth Corp) while their parents looked on, the gasoline-soaked bus burst into flames. Up in arms about integration, the Klan burned the bus in opposition of a recent federal court-ordered, school busing plan.

When the Imperial Wizard stepped forward to speak, an enthusiastic crowd hailed him. According to a Klan newspaper, Wilkinson told the crowd of about 600, "People in the North and South are opposed to busing children to achieve racial balance in schools." He urged whites in Decatur to join forces with them to help stop the busing.

When he got through speaking, flames of a seventy-foot cross lit the night sky. The group cheered.

"Okay, all you little nigger kids can come out of the bus now," a man yelled.

Together they all laughed with reverberating merriment, "let 'em burn!"[11]

---

[11] (Night in Alabama With the Ku Klux Klan 1979)

CHAPTER 15

What Do You See

"One could see he (Tommy Hines) is mentally retarded. I can't see why he is in prison and not in a mental hospital," an international jurist remarked.[1] Invited to the United States to tour prisons and investigate charges of human rights violations, the two men visited Alabama's Kilby prison in early August, 1979.[2] That report, in addition to a complaint of abuse filed by Hines' attorney, led to an investigation. A month earlier, Tommy's father, SCLC leaders, and his attorney, U. W. Clemon, visited the prison. Hines was thin and wearing glasses, somewhat withdrawn; he scribbled something on a paper and said, "they the five who did it."[3] Kilby officials denied that the inmate had been raped and beaten.

Accusations of alleged ill-treatment started a campaign. Governor Fob James received numerous phone calls and letters from private citizens, community groups, legislative members, prison and civil rights organizations. The crusade forced the governor to order a psychological exam. A three-member sanity committee was appointed to review Hine's mental state. After an examination, Dr. Robert Estock, psychiatrist at the University of Alabama at Birmingham, wrote "In my opinion, the patient is suffering from a mental illness in addition to his severe mental retardation. I would diagnose him as having a schizophrenic reaction-catatonic type in partial remission." He further stated that Hines' condition was exacerbated by imprisonment. The doctor theorized that his "periods of withdrawal, muteness, and rigid posturing and failure to

---

[1] (Johnston 1979)
[2] (Blanchard 1979)
[3] (After Visit With Hines, SCLC Leaders Believe He's Innocent of Rape 1979)

respond to questions to periods of agitation and prolonged screaming started in July after reports of abuse...There have also been periods of refusal to eat, as well as periods of incontinence (an inability to control urination)."[4]

As a result of the panel's evaluation, a formal recommendation to institutionalize Hines prompted Governor James to order a committal.[5] On Oct. 17, the young man was checked into Bryce Hospital at Tuscaloosa. This action did not, however, hinder further trial proceedings or affect any appeals.

Five months later, an Alabama Court of Criminal Appeals reversed the rape conviction. It unanimously ruled that Hines did not receive a fair trial. The young man's parents hoped to have their son safe and back with them. "I want my boy home," Mrs. Hines declared.[6]

The state attorney general filed a petition and asked that the court's decision be reviewed.

Although Klansmen were just three blocks away, a peaceful civil rights march took place on May 26, 1980, two years after Tommy's arrest and a year after the shooting melee in Decatur. SCLC members left the church and walked to the spot where the confrontation had taken place. They sang and prayed. Petitioning the Lord, the Reverend Abraham Woods, president of the Birmingham chapter of SCLC, prayed, "We have come to this spot to let Decatur know that we are not afraid and to tell those who fired the shots that they cannot put out the freedom fire."[7]

The civil rights group then walked to City Hall. Whites, some outfitted in Klan dress, stood across the street, observing the marchers' every move. This time, no gunfire and no violent confrontation occurred.

After the Alabama Supreme Court upheld the Court of Appeals decision, one of Hines' attorneys, Oscar Adams, Jr. (a partner in the

---

[4] (L. Elliott 1979)
[5] (AP, Hines Has Been Moved 1979)
[6] (Jet 1980)
[7] (AP, SCLC, Klan March Peacefully 1980)

firm with Clemon), filed a petition for his client to be released. Adams' request was based on the fact that the governor's order was no longer valid since hospital officials had established in July that his client did not need hospitalization.[8]

Tommy's few belongings were packed in a small suitcase. Free on a $10,000 bond, the man left the insane asylum on August 25, 1980. He returned home to the protective custody of his family. He was different though. After spending a year in prison and 10 months in a mental institution, Tommy was quiet and distant. While his family rallied around him with love and attempts to return things to normal, he didn't eat or drink much. He didn't talk much. Within six weeks of being home, he had lost 30 pounds and had to be rushed to Decatur General Hospital. His diagnosis was dehydration.[9]

Hearing about Hines' condition, Jefferson County Judge Charles Crowder ordered him to the psychiatric unit of the University Hospital at Birmingham. A competency hearing was scheduled for November.

On Monday, September 29, a trial began in Decatur accusing Curtis Robinson with "assault with intent to murder." A jury of six women and six men had been selected. Months earlier, Judge Hundley had rejected a change of venue motion.

Shortly after the May 1979 shooting, Robinson had sought legal counsel from Clint Brown. The Decatur attorney contacted Morris Dees at the Southern Poverty Law Center in Montgomery, Alabama.[10] Brown handed the phone to Robinson, who begged Dees to take his case. After hearing more details about the shooting, the Montgomery lawyer was so attracted by the case that he visited Decatur and agreed to represent the defendant.[11]

During court, Robinson claimed self-defense in the shooting of

---

[8] (AP, Attorney Seeks Hines Release 1980)
[9] (Hines in Stable Condition 1980)
[10] The Southern Poverty Law Center was founded by attorneys Morris Dees and Joe Levin. The firm was dedicated to handling antidiscrimination cases.
[11] (Dees 2001)

David Kelso. Footage had been obtained by his attorney that showed Kelso provoked Robinson.

Testifying on his behalf, Robinson recounted the event and told how the Klan had blocked the marchers, breaking through the police line. In a fury, he said that they rushed on the protestors, attacking with clubs and bats. When robed white men bashed his car with his wife Eva and children inside, Robinson said he grabbed his .38 revolver, and jumped out of the car.[12] About nine Klansmen ran toward him, shouting racial obscenities. He fired, and then turned and ran.[13] Robinson told jurors that his family had narrowly escaped. Later, when he returned to get his car, he revealed that it was badly banged up. A front tire and headlight had also been shot out.

District Attorney Mike Moebes argued that Robinson's firing his gun, spurred the skirmish that led to four people being shot.

The all-white jury found Curtis Robinson "guilty." Judge Hundley sentenced the defendant to five years in prison, but adhering to the jury's recommendation, he suspended the sentence and granted two-years' probation.[14] Robinson was the first African American man ever to go on trial for attacking a Klansman. Subsequently, his attorney stated, "This verdict makes history in this state and this nation because it's the first time a black man has ever been convicted of shooting a robed Klansman who advanced on him with a raised club."[15]

Lawyer Dees appealed the conviction. Furthermore, in an unprecedented move, the Southern Poverty Law Center filed a one million dollar federal law suit against the Klan, its leader and several members who were involved in the 1979 confrontation.[16]

Continuing to prosecute Tommy Hines for the first rape case, Mike Moebes filed a motion for a new trial. Judge Jack Riley, once again, moved the case from Cullman to Birmingham.

---

[12] (Robinson v State 1983)
[13] (AP, Judge Sentences Black Man in Wounding of Klansman 1980)
[14] (Robinson v State 1983)
[15] (Dees 2001)
[16] Ibid.

As Hines' competency court date approached, attorney Demetrius Newton filed a motion for the judge – not a jury – to consider whether or not his client was fit to stand trial.[17] Judge Crowder denied the request. When court opened on November 17, 1980, security was tight in and around the Jefferson County courthouse. Metal detectors had recently been installed, anticipating danger.

Eight women, one of them black, and four men were selected as jurors. The justice admonished the panel that they were "not to consider Hines' guilty or innocent but only whether he can understand the charges against him and is capable of helping his attorneys prepare his defense."[18]

Doctors who examined Hines gave conflicting testimony. The psychiatrist at Bryce Hospital, Dr. James Thompson, testified that Hines knew he was charged with rape and that he described the three crimes. Thompson also said that the accused had a fair understanding of the court proceedings and that he was competent to stand trial.

A loud and unexpected outburst shocked and even startled courtroom observers. Interrupting Dr. Thompson's testimony, Hines muttered unintelligible sounds, as he shook his head back and forth and smiled from ear to ear. He let out another loud garbled sound. Rapping his gavel, the judge dismissed the jury and warned Hines to be quiet.[19]

Dr. Lloyd Baccus, a psychiatrist for the defense testified that Hines "had the mind of a five-year old with no concept of sexual relationship and should not stand trial." He described him as being suggestible. "Tommy would respond to the individual he thought was in authority and he wished to please," he conveyed.

Defense attorney Newton stood to deliver his closing argument.

---

[17] Demetrius Newton was a civil rights attorney and politician. He filed lawsuits to end segregation, and represented Martin Luther King, Jr., Rosa Parks, and others in cases related to civil rights. He was elected to the Alabama House of Representatives in 1986. In 1998, Newton became the first Black speaker pro tempore in the history of the Alabama House, serving in the role from 1998 through 2010. (Source: Wikipedia).

[18] (Hayes, Jurors Ponder Hines 1980)

[19] (AP, Hine's Hearing Continues 1990)

What Do You See

Confidently, he offered a thin smile and opened by telling the jurors a story:

> The Master met a man on the street and asked him, "What is your name?" The man said his name was Legion because he was filled with a legion of demons, and his devils were many. The Master cast out the demons and told him to go back to his kinfolk and friends and let them know about the good thing that had happened to him. Nobody has suggested here that Tommy Lee Hines was an animal. He's a sick person, but he's not an animal. Some have argued here that he ought to be another Legion. But I'm glad there are still people in the world who are willing to say, "Yes, your devils are many, but we're going to take this opportunity to do what we know to be right."

A fifteen-minute psychiatric examination video was permitted by the court. Both Mike Moebes and Burton Dunn, Jefferson County, objected. The video revealed significant facts about the abilities of the twenty-eight year old:

- A verdict is a lady who just had a baby.
- There are 60 hours in a day.
- Sometimes a judge puts you in jail for something you haven't done.
- A jury and a judge are the same thing.
- One pencil plus one pencil equals three pencils.
- September, October, November and December are days of the week.
- There are 65 pennies in a dime.

"That tape you saw was Tommy at his very best," Newton hammered. He went on to tell the jury that after 10 years of testing, his client had the mind of a "five-year old adult imbecile." As he ended his summation, the trial lawyer studied the jurors' faces. Looking each one directly in the eyes, he lowered his voice, his hands moved in sync with his words.

"What is your name? My name is Legion, for my devils are many. Find Tommy Lee Hines incompetent and cast out the devils."[20] Newton sat down.

Next, the prosecutor stood to present his closing argument. With tears in his eyes and a cracking voice, Mike Moebes appealed to the jurors:

> They want to tell you that there's no way he could remember the factual details of the event with which he is charged, yet the same man tells you that he (Hines) told him about two occasions when he was raped himself.
>
> If he can recall how he was raped twice, then how in the world can that doctor say he couldn't also recall the events with which he is charged? They tell you one thing and then they turn around and tell you something else. It's not right. It's just not right.
>
> This defendant for 25 years was retarded, but ask yourself this question. For 25 years, what did he do? He lived in society. He functioned in society. He understood what rape was. Granted, he's retarded, but he knew what rape was and he knew that if you 12 find him competent then he's going to stand trial and that if he's tried and found guilty, he'll go to prison. If he's tried and found innocent, he'll go home.

---

[20] (Hayes, Jurors Ponder Hines 1980)

What Do You See

Drawing attention to the contradictory expert testimony, Morgan County's DA continued:

> I've dealt for years and years with psychiatrists. The best analogy I know of is, they're like vending machines. If you put peanuts in 'em, they'll spit out peanuts. If you put cheese crackers in 'em, they'll spit out cheese crackers. If you put Cracker Jacks in 'em, they'll spit out Cracker Jacks.[21]

Attacking the video, the prosecutor called it "plain, common, pure quackery." "Objection!" Newton shouted several times. Moebes pointed out that the tape was made at the suggestion of Hines' attorneys. "It is nothing but a contrived, preconceived piece of garbage. It's a set-up, ladies and gentlemen, and I submit to you that you better show the defense lawyers across the state and nation that at least juries in Jefferson County are not going to go along with this."[22] He completed his closing argument.

The jury deliberated only two hours before reaching a verdict: "Unfit to stand trial." Judge Crowder signed an order to commit Tommy, first to Bryce and then to Partlow Mental Health Institution, until he was competent to stand trial.

"I'm proud they freed my son for something he didn't do. They have dogged him for three years," Hines' father said. "I'm proud they did the right thing for him. That boy can't stand no trial. I want him at my house. I can take care of him. I don't want him to go to no kind of institution."[23] Contrary to what many believed, the decision was not about the defendant's guilt or innocence but his intellectual ability.

Highly upset about the verdict, Moebes vowed to consult with State Attorney General Graddick to pursue reinstatement. "I intend to

---

[21] Ibid.
[22] Ibid.
[23] (UPI, Prosecutor Seeks Retardant's Trial 1980)

take every step that I consider reasonable in prosecuting this case," he swore.[24]

Nearly ten years after the Southern Poverty Law Center brought its suit against Klansmen (Bernice Brown v The Invisible Empire, Knights of Ku Klux Klan, etc., et al.) who were involved in the Decatur shooting, the defendants were sentenced and fined. U.S. District Court judge Elbert B. Haltom ordered five of the men "not to be a member of the Klan for ten years, another for two years." They were to refrain from "committing and conspiring to commit acts of violence, intimidation, harassment, or assault upon any black person." The judge further charged eight of the white supremacists to pay fines in varying amounts. In addition, five of the Klansmen were ordered to attend a race relations seminar, led by Dr. Joseph Lowery and other civil rights leaders.[25]

On May 12, 1990, a two-hour class was held at the Ramada Inn Civic Center in Birmingham. Four of the five ordered to attend the class showed up. Media outlets had asked to be present, but Dr. Lowery declined their request. During the session, SCLC's National President imparted "the oneness of the human family, forgiveness and more."[26]

"Partlow has become a symbol of neglect, a warehouse for casting off humanity, sentenced to life without hope of contact with the rest of us. It took a federal court order to loosen encrusted bureaucracy and free Alabama's mental health system."[27] This sentiment printed in an editorial in *The Montgomery Advertiser* in 1983, summed up the atrocious conditions of the mental health facility.

The following year, Tommy Hines' counsel, Demetrius Newton, filed a motion to quash the Morgan County indictments of raping three women and robbery. Hines' attorney said, "The flaw in the state statues means his mentally retarded client will end up spending the

---

[24] Ibid.
[25] (Brown v The Invisible Empire, Knights of the Ku Klux Klan 1989)
[26] (Lowery 2011)
[27] (Editorial 1983)

rest of his life in an institution because he'll never be fit for trial."[28] Citing Alabama statues, he commented that, "Under our state law, and especially the insanity statue, we do very little with mentally retarded person like Mr. Hines, who is not insane, he's just mentally retarded." Newton further affirmed, "We (the state of Alabama) just don't have anything in the law to deal with incompetent people as opposed to insane (people)...Tommy is not a criminal, he's just an unfortunate retarded young black man and there's little hope of his ever attaining normalcy."

The motion was rejected.

Later, when Partlow began deinstitutionalizing, Tommy Hines was moved to a state certified group home for individuals with intellectual and developmental disabilities. He learned some life skills, participated in day programs, and often offered to assist with other duties. The residential facility would be his home until February 11, 2020.

---

[28] (AP, Attorney Says Flaw Confines Hines to State Institution 1984)

Epilogue

The summer of 1978 changed Decatur, Alabama. Prior to this time, however, the age-old virus of racism had metamorphosed itself. Every section of the city and county was exposed. While widespread, its subtleness in some instances, prompted citizens to deny existence of the horrible destructiveness of the disease. The deadly virus reached epidemic proportion after the arrest and conviction of Tommy Lee Hines, Decatur's Scapegoat.

Nearly a decade later, the city's mayor, Bill Dukes could reflect on the peak level that had occurred in 1979, and left four people wounded. He could also appreciate the fact that the curve was bending. Special efforts made to unite the River City and bring jobs to the municipality were positive. Several blacks had been appointed to boards and worked in offices downtown. Russell Priest had been appointed in 1986 to serve on the city council. No black had functioned in that capacity since 1894. Modification of districts guaranteed black representation. Transportation to bus students was available and school tensions that once stemmed from integration had all but ceased, as students learned that they had more in common than not. Race relations were a work in progress.

In 2020, forty-two years since Hines' arrest, breakthroughs in racial equity have continued to enrich the city. Today, opportunities for citizens in Decatur and Morgan County are more equitable. Still, residents are faced with challenges, some more elusive than ever before. Outbreaks do flare up, and as with most viruses the sickness of systemic racism and ethnic disparities often hits hard and spreads quickly. People with changed hearts and renewed spirits, can continue to make strides, be better people, stand up for the moral rights of others, and be a voice, as many did for "Brother Tommy."

Tragically, the story of Tommy Lee Hines' misfortune has all but escaped the memory of many people. The unfortunate circumstances of Decatur's Scapegoat, however, should never be forgotten. Tommy Hines was the catalyst that not only exposed racial disparities but also significantly improved community relations (politically, religiously, economically, and educationally). Tommy Hines was the spark needed to spur all to look deep into their own consciences, to examine the moral character of their actions. In some real way, he was the laboratory that tested racial inequalities and marked the start of a long healing process. As Marvin Dinsmore so poignantly put it, "Most of us knew he was innocent. Why, Tommy couldn't even put a key in a car door, let alone drive it. But the sad thing about it all, his real situation got lost in all the hullabaloo."[29] Yes, the true cause may have gotten lost, but gains to the city have been invaluable.

Tommy Hines, Decatur's Scapegoat, suffered from the anguish of being falsely accused and convicted, prison abuse, and years of separation from his family, all detrimental to his health and well-being. His last visit home was in 1986 when he attended his mother's funeral. After his parents' death, family members attempted to locate him. For a very long time, they were unsuccessful in even finding out exactly where he was, but now they know.

The Tuscaloosa death notice was simple. It read:

Thomas Lee Hines

OCTOBER 10, 1952 – FEBRUARY 11, 2020
Thomas Lee Hines was born on October 10, 1952
and passed away on February 11, 2020 and is under
the care of Heritage Chapel Funeral Home.
Graveside Service will be held on February 21, 2020
at 2:00 pm at Sunset Memorial Park.[30]

---

[29] (Perske 1991)
[30] (Heritage Chapel Funeral Home 2020)

Bibliography

Brown v The Invisible Empire, Knights of the Ku Klux Klan. CV 80-1449 (The United States District Court for the Northern District of Alabama Southern Division, November 21, 1989).
n.d.
AP. "Attorney Seeks Hines Release." *Alabama Journal*, August 13, 1980.
—. "Dozen Witnesses Likely to Testify on Hines' Behalf." *Alabama Journal*, October 11, 1978: 2.
—. "Hines Stands Trial for Rape in Alabama." *Casper Star-Tribune*, October 4, 1978: 6.
—. "Attorney Says Flaw Confines Hines to State Institution." *The Alabama Journal*, February 23, 1984: 4.
—. "Hines Raped Her, Woman Testifies." *The Alabama Journal*, October 3, 1978: 1.
—. "Hine's Hearing Continues." *The Anniston Star*, November 19, 1990: 6.
—. "Hines Judge Stress Impartiality." *The Anniston Star*, 5 1978, October: 1.
—. "KKK Members Defy Weapons Ban." *The Anniston Star*, February 25, 1979: 8.
—. "SCLC, Klan March Peacefully." *The Anniston Star*, May 27, 1980: 5B.
—. "Blacks March to Trial Falls Back." *The Montgomery Advertiser*, October 2, 1978: 2.
—. "Bomb Threat Clears Court in Cullman Rape Trial." *The Montgomery Advertiser*, October 5, 1978: 18.
—. "Judge Sentences Black Man in Wounding of Klansman." *The Montgomery Advertiser*, October 3, 1980: 22.
—. "Hines Has Been Moved." *The Selma Times*, October 18, 1979: 24.

—. "Jury Gets Hines Hearing." *The Selma Times Journal*, November 21, 1980: 3.

—. "Hines Trial May Go To Jury Today." *The Selma Times-Journal*, October 13, 1978: 10.

—. "Blacks, Klan in Standoff." *The Shrievport Journal*, October 3, 1978: 2A.

Blanchard, Frank. "Hines To Have More Testing." *Montgomery Advertiser*, August 30, 1979: 15.

Burns, Tony. "Bomb Calls Delay Trial; Court Security Tightens." *The Cullman Times*, October 5, 1978: 1.

—. "Rape Case May Go to Jurors By Weekend, Attorneys Predict." *The Cullman Times*, October 12, 1978: 1.

—. "Rape Victim Points Out Hines as Assailant in February Attack." *The Cullman Times*, October 4, 1978: 5.

Cable, Veronica, interview by Peggy Towns. *Marcher and SCLC Member* (September 2, 2019).

Cantrell, Wanda. "Cullman Talks of Trial." *The Montgomery Advertiser*, October 6, 1978: 2.

—. "Hines Case Attorneys Squabbling." *The Montgomery Advertiser*, November 15, 1978: 1.

—. "Hines Defense Begins." *The Montgomery Advertiser*, October 11, 1978: 1.

—. "Hines Defense Rest." *The Montgomery Advertiser*, October 13, 1978: 2.

—. "Hines Lawyer Agree To Join Forces." *The Montgomery Advertiser*, January 6, 1979: 3.

—. "Tommy Hines gets 30 years." *The Montgomery Advertiser*, October 14, 1978: 5.

Clemon, U W. "Making Bricks Without Straw: The NAACP Legal Defense Fund and the Development of Civil Rights Law in Alabama 1940-1980." *Alabama Law Review*, 2001.

Cullman Times Democrat. "Federal Authorities Checking Beating of Black Man Locally." December 21, 1978: 1.

Dart, Bob. "Cullman, Alabama feels Trial of Textbook Southern Justice: ." *The Atlanta Constitution*, October 13, 1978: 28.

—. "Father, Tommy Lee Belongs Right Here." *The Atlanta Constitution*, April 2, 1980: 6A.

—. "No Sir, Only Words From Hines At Trial." *The Atlanta Constitution*, April 1, 1980: 12.

Decatur Daily. "Blacks March For Cullman." October 1, 1978: 1.

Decatur Daily. "Plea of Hines Shocks Backers." September 2, 1978: 1.

Decatur Daily. "Victorious Blacks Set New Goals." August 19, 1977: 2.

Dees, Morris, Fiffer, Steve. *A Lawyer's Journey. The Morris Dees Story*. Chicago: American Bar Association, 2001.

Department, Decatur Police. Police Timeline, Decatur, 1978.

Donnavant, Bob. "Bomb Threat Delays Alabama Rape Trial." *The Tennesseean*, October 1978, 1978: 60.

Dunnavant, Bob. "Confession Account Gets Judge's Nod." *The Tennessean*, October 10, 1978: 24.

—. "Alabama Rape Confession Recalled." *The Tennessean*, October 4, 1978: 18.

—. "Cullman State Set for Klan, Black Faceoff." *The Tennessean*, December 22, 1978: 14.

—. "Defense Lawyers Rest Hines Case." *The Tennessean*, October 13, 1978: 27.

—. "'Good Boy' Hines Gets 30 Years for Rape in Alabama." *The Tennessean*, October 14, 1978: 4.

—. "Klan Attacks Marchers. Gunfire Marks Decatur Battle." *The Tennessean*, Ma 28, 1979: 1.

—. "Klanman Met: Blacks Marching in Rape Charge Protest Taunted." *The Tennessean*, October 2, 1978: 1.

—. "Klansman Met. Blacks Marching in Rape Charge Protest Taunted." *The Tennessean*, October 2, 1978: 10.

—. "Psycologist's View Sought. Witness Challenged in Rape Trial." *The Tennessean*, October 6, 1978: 4.

—. "Rape Defense Loses Argument. Written Confession Allowed." *The Tennessean*, October 11, 1978: 16.

Editorial. "Same Song." *The Montgomery Advertiser*, February 15, 1983: 4.

Editors, Biography.com. *Ralph D. Abernathy Biography*. January 17, 2020. https://www.biography.com/activist/ralph-d-abernathy (accessed March 21, 2020).

Elliott, Ernestine Bell, interview by Peggy Towns. *Tommy Hines* (March 31, 2020).

Elliott, Lou. "Hines Ordered to Institution." *Alabama Journal*, October 11, 1979: 2.

Field, Jeff. "Civil Rights Leaders March on City Hall; Abernathy Pledges Support for Hines." *Decatur Daily*, August 16, 1978: 1.

—. "Klan Members Burn Cross at City Hall: Blacks March." *Decatur Daily*, August 15, 1978: 1.

—. "Lawyer for Hines Challenges Order Sending Him to Bryce." *Decatur Daily*, June 27, 1978: 1.

—. "Some 500 Blacks March on City Hall." *Decatur Daily*, May 30, 1978: 1.

—. "Broader Support Asked for Hines." *The Decatur Daily*, October 24, 1978: 1.

—. "Hundreds Came to Join Tommy Hines March." *The Decatur Daily*, June 10, 1979: A-5.

Fields, Jeff. "Judge begins Jury Selection; Walk Resumes." *Decatur Daily*, October 2, 1978.

Fields, Jeff, and Wayne Morgan. "Over 1000 Watch Klan Burn Cross." *Decatur Daily*, July 15, 1978: 1.

Foreman, Paul. "SCLC, Klan Marches Peaceful Here." *The Decatur Daily*, June 10, 1979: 2.

Guster, J, interview by Peggy Towns. *Hines Marches* (September 9, 2019).

Guster, T, interview by Peggy Towns. *Tommy Hines Marches* (June 30, 2020).

Hayes, Drew. "Jurors Ponder Hines." *The Decatur Daily*, November 21, 1980: 1, 5.

—. "Klan Stayed Off Street During March by Blacks." *The Decatur Daily*, June 10, 1979: A5.

Hayes, Drew, and Jeff Field. "Klansman Shooting Charged to Man." *The Decatur Daily*, May 29, 1979: 1.

Hayes, Drew, Cathy D Wahl, and Morgan Wayne. "More Arrests Possible in Race Melee As Police Probe Shootings of 4 Here." *The Decatur Daily*, May 27, 1979: 1,14.

Heritage Chapel Funeral Home. 2020. https://www.dignitymemorial.com/obituaries/tuscaloosa-al/thomas-hines-9044835 (accessed July 1, 2020).

Hill, University of North Carolina at Chapel. *Seeking4Truth*. 2004. http://www.seeking4truth.com/centennial_encyclopaedia.htm (accessed July 27, 2020).

Hines v. State,. 384 So. 2d 1171 (Court of Criminal Appeals of Alabama, April 22, 1980).

Jet.April 10, 1980: 7.

Jet. "a." n.d.

Jet. "After Visit With Hines, SCLC Leaders Believe He's Innocent of Rape." July 26, 1979: 8.

Johnston, Rhodes. "Jurist Impressed by Harris, Hines." *Alabama Journal, Montgomery Alabama*, August 10, 1979: 1.

Kahn, Joseph. "Southern Justice." *The New York Times*, March 2, 1979: 19.

King, Wayne. "Two Klansmen And Black Women Are Shot In A Street Clash In Alabama." *The New York Times*, May 27, 1979: 26.

Longview News Journal. "Hines Incapable of Understand His Legal Rights." October 5, 1978: 7.

Lowery, Joseph H. *Singing The Lord's Song In A Strange Land*. Nashville: Abingdon Press, 2011.

Miranda Rights. 2020. http://www.mirandarights.org/ (accessed May 17, 2020).

Morse, Pamela. "Rape Victim Identifies Hines As Her Assailant." *Decatur Daily*, October 3, 1978: 1.

Morton, Jason. "Bryce Hospital Established Tuscaloosa as Center of Mental Health Care." *The Tuscaloosa News*, December 31, 2019.

Perske, Robert. *Unequalled Justice: What Can Happen With Retardation Or Other Developmental Disabilities Encounter The Criminal Justice System*. Nashville: Abingdon Press, 1991.

Press, Associated. "Rape Victim Identifies Hines as Attacker." *The Clarion-Ledger*, October 4, 1978: 6.

Protestors Are Given Trial Date.February 12, 1979: 1.

Robinson v State. 430 So. 2d 883 (Ala. Crim. App. 1983) (Court of Criminal Appeals of Alabama, May 6, 1983).

Scott-McLaughlin, Randolph M., Betty Lawrence Bailey, and Yvette Torres-Frankel. *Racially-motivated Violence: Litigation Strategies*. New York: Center for Constitutional Rights, 1984.

Sheriff, Department of. "Arrest reports after Hundley's order." Chronical of arrest, Decatur, 1978.

Sherill, James. "SCLC and Klan clash." Investigator's report, Decatur, Alabama, 1979.

Sorin, Gretchen. *Driving While Black African American Travel and the Road to Civil Rights*. New York, February 11, 2020.

State of Alabama vs Tommy Lee Hines. CC78-0340H, CC78-0341-H, CC78-0342H, CC78-0343H (Circuit Court for Morgan County, August 16, 1978).

Suggs, Ernie. "A 'Special Woman' Who Made History." *The Atlanta Journal Constitution*, September 27, 2013.

Taylor, Ron. "Drama Growing in Hines Trial, but Air of Confrontation Eases." *The Atlanta Constitution*, October 8, 1978: 2.

The Albany, Decatur Daily. "Columbus Union Names its Officers." April 6, 1919: 3.

The Anniston Star. "FBI Sent to Decatur After Saturday Racial Shootings." May 28, 1979: 2A.

The Decatur Daily. "Cullman Scene of Demonstration." December 22, 1978: 1.

The Decatur Daily. "Hines in Stable Condition." October 8, 1980: 1.

The Decatur Daily. "Hines out on bale, declared competent." July 15, 1978.

The Decatur Daily. "Whites in Cullman Angry About Trial." October 5, 1978: 1.

The New York Times. "Judge Moves Rape Trial of Hines to Birmingham." March 3, 1979: 21.

The New York Times. "Klan Leader Admits Attack on Black Minister." December 21, 1978.

The News and Observe, Raleigh, North Carolina. "Klan admits Black's Abduction." December 21, 1978: 15.

The Selma Times Journal. "Huntsville-An Attorney Representing." November 5, 1978: 2.

The Washington Post. "Night in Alabama With the Ku Klux Klan." August 26, 1979.

Times, Special to the New York. "Rights Group Agree on Lawyers In Retarded Man's Rape Appeal." *New York Times*, January 6, 1979: 7.

Turner, Sonny. "SCLC, Klan Prepared for City Marches." *The Decatur Daily*, June 9, 1979: 1.

UPI. "Father: Son Home Night of Rape." *The Boston Globe*, October 12, 1978: 1978.

—. "Rape Trial Continues." *The Daily News-Journal (Murfreesboro Teneessee)*, October 6, 1978: 14.

—. "Threats Interrupt Retarded Man's Trial." *The Greenville News*, October 5, 1978: 9-A.

—. "Prosecutor Seeks Retardant's Trial." *The Indianapolis Star*, Nov 23, 1980: 13.

—. "He Can't Understand Rights Court is Told." *The Miami Herald*, October 6, 1978: 9.

Wahl, Cathy D. "Hines Receives Word on His Legal Rights." *Decatur Daily*, June 6, 1978: 1.

—. "Hines Said 'He Had Sex' - Consultant." *Decatur Daily*, October 6, 1978.

Wahl, Cathy. "Hines' Defense Could End Today." *Decatur Daily (Valley Edition)*, October 12, 1978.

—. "Blacks exhorted by SCLC chief'." *Decatur Daily*, July 8, 1978: 1.

—. "Hines is Indicted Moved to Tuscaloosa." *Decatur Daily*, June 24, 1978: 1.

—. "Judge Allows Jury to Hear Confession." *Decatur Daily*, October 9, 1978: 1.

—. "Witnesses Testify Hines' is Innoncent." *Decatur Daily*, October 11, 1978: A-10.

—. "Tommy Hines Case Expected to Reach Jury Today." *The Decatur Daily*, October 13, 1978: 1.

Whal, Cathy. "Hines Case on the way to Grand Jury." *Decatur Daily*, June 24, 1978: 1.

Wikipedia. *U. W. Clemon*. November 5, 2019. https://en.wikipedia.org/wiki/U._W._Clemon (accessed July 10, 2020).

Index

Symbols

14th Amendment 19, 90

A

Abernathy, Ralph 34, 35, 50
    Over 1500 Hines' supporters march 101
Adams, Oscar Jr. 107, 108
African People's Socialist 101
Alabama Black Caucus 101
Alabama Jubilee 29
Allen, Cynthia xi, 98
Allen, George xi, 15, 133
Allen, Myrtle 98, 105
Allen Petrina 98
Anderson, Jack R. 55, 56, 67, 68
A&P Supermarket 88
Arc of Morgan County 8
Automatic Screw 2, 60

B

Baccus, Lloyd 110
Bell, Griffin 97
Black Caucus 97, 101
Bland, Julian 49
BOMB 54
Bowman 88
Brookhaven Middle School 69
Brown, Bernice 7, 8, 94, 114
Brown, Clint 108
Bryant, Bear 85
Bryce Hospital 19, 58, 61, 71, 107, 110
Busby, Charles 2

Busy Bee Market 97

C

Carrie Matthews Recreation Center 98
Carter, Jimmy 85
Chairs, James 94, 95
Change of Venue 54, 65, 89
Change of venue granted
    Unprecedented move in Alabama History 90, 91
Charlotte Equal Rights Council 101
Cherry Street School Developmental Center 4, 68
City Hall 6, 13, 14, 15, 16, 61, 91, 104, 107
Clark, Robert 52, 62
Clemon, U. W. 85, 86, 91
    Prison visit and investigtion initiated 106
Coggins. Thomas 21
Concerned Parents Committee 9
Conyers, John 97
Cook Sergeant 22
Cottonreader 10, 11, 12, 14, 16, 20, 21, 22, 24, 30, 41, 44, 81, 87, 88, 89, 92, 95
    Burned court order 21
    Organization of Morgan County SCLC 14
    Over 1500 Hines' supporters march 101
    Speaks to over 1500 103
Cottonreader, R. B. xii, 15, 20
    March on DA's house 20

Cottonreader, R. B. arrested 29
cross burning 17, 31, 32, 100
cross burning and bus burning 105
Cross, Jerry 69
Crowder, Charles
    Back to psychiatric unit 108
    Committment order signed 113
Cullman City Limits 44, 46
Cullman County 41, 47, 49
    Billed Morgan County for trial 86

D

Daily, Cora 18, 55
Decatur xi, xiv, 4, 5, 7, 8, 9, 10, 12, 13, 14, 15, 17, 18, 22, 26, 29, 30, 31, 32, 44, 47, 60, 63, 87, 88, 89, 91, 97, 105, 108, 114, 117, 118, 133
Dees, Morris 109
    Filed million dollar law suit against Klan 109
Dinsmore, Marvin xii, 8, 9, 18, 58, 118
Dukes, Bill 13, 14, 16, 89, 97
    Reflections 117
Dunlap, Tim 18, 68, 69
Dunn, Burton 111

E

Effigy 92
Estock, Robert 106

F

Fauntroy, Walter 101, 104
Federal Justice Department 97
First Baptist Church 29, 84
Floyd, George xiii
Ford, Johnny
    Over 1500 Hines' supporters march 101
    Speaks to crowd of over 1500 104
Ford, June 23, 29

Forrest, Nathan Bedford 31
Fuqua, Latonya 42

G

Garth, Catherine 8
Garth, Donny 97
Godfrey, Deran 95
Goodloe, Percy 15
Gordon, Pat 69
Graddick, Charlie
    Alabama Supreme Court request to intervene 90
    Petition Alabama Court of Criminal Appeals 90
Guster, James xii, 44, 82, 94, 95
Guster, Timothy 94

H

Hairston, George 41, 45, 49, 51, 58, 62, 64, 65, 70, 71, 72, 73
    Cross-examines Doyle Ward 63
    Cross-examines Dr. Edwin Seger 72
    Cross-examines Dr. Thomas Smith 70
Highway 24 32
Hines 106
    Competency hearing 110
    Death notice 115
    Free on bond, 1980 108
    Motion to quash 114
    Over 1500 Hines' supporters 84, 95, 96, 98
    Panel's recommendation to institutionalize 107
    Report from International Jurist 106
Hines, Bessie 4, 44, 107
Hines, Billy 8
Hines, Richard 4, 10, 19, 53, 82, 113

Hines, Tommy vii, xi, xii, xiv, 2, 3, 4,
  7, 8, 10, 12, 13, 14, 15, 16, 17,
  18, 19, 21, 23, 25, 26, 29, 30, 31,
  32, 41, 42, 44, 45, 49, 50, 51,
  52, 53, 54, 55, 56, 57, 58, 59,
  60, 61, 62, 63, 64, 65, 66, 67,
  68, 69, 70, 71, 72, 73, 74, 75,
  76, 82, 84, 85, 86, 88, 89, 91,
  92, 98, 103, 106, 108, 110, 113,
  115, 117, 118
  Alabama Court of Criminal
    Appeals reversed rape
    conviction 107
  Alabama Supreme Court upheld
    decision 107
  Closing Argument by Newton 111
  Committment order signed 113
  Mental age 4.6 89
  Verdict of guilty 75
Holmes, Allen 69
Holmes, Alvin 101
Holmes, Maggie 9, 18, 55
Holyfield, Paxton 42
H., Rosemary 45
Hundley, Richard 19, 21, 36, 37,
  108, 109

J

James, Fob Jr. 97, 106
Jim Crow laws 31
Jones, Floyd 6, 69, 70
Justice City 16

K

Kelso, David 94, 97, 109
Kilgo, Berdice 94
King, Dr. Martin Luther King, Jr. 9,
  15, 16, 29, 50, 110
Kirk, Jackie 23
Kirk, Larry xii, 15, 20, 22, 23, 24, 30,
  41, 43, 44, 76

Over 1500 Hines' supporters
  march 101
Kirk, Larry arrested 29
Klan xiv, 17, 28, 31, 32, 44, 45, 48, 75,
  87, 88, 89, 91, 92, 93, 94, 95,
  96, 100, 102, 104, 105, 109, 114

L

Lacon 43
Lee, Bernard
  Over 1500 Hines' supporters
    march 101
Legion 111
Leland, Mickey 101
Loftin, Joel 57, 58, 66, 67
Lowery, Dr. Joseph E. 26, 29, 30, 46,
  47, 77, 84, 85, 91, 94, 95, 96, 97,
  102, 114
  Court ordered class for Klan 114
  Over 1500 Hines' supporters
    march 101
Lowery, Evelyn 30, 81
  Vehicle shot up 94
Lurleen B. Wallace Center 57, 66

M

Marshall, Eddie 6, 69, 70
Martin. Lorene 9, 16, 50, 110
Mays, Veronica 15
McDaniel, Ida McDaniel 50
McGlocklin, Bill 87
Mims, Henry 9, 15, 19, 41, 45, 49, 54,
  55, 61, 67, 72, 74, 85, 86, 90
  Direct Cross of Dr. Jack
    Henderson 67
Miranda 51, 52, 55, 56, 58, 61, 66, 67,
  70, 72
Moebes
  Closing argument 112

Moebes, Mike 17, 18, 19, 20, 30, 49, 50, 54, 56, 57, 58, 59, 68, 69, 71, 73, 74, 90, 109, 113
   Cross-examines Dr. Henson 66
   Questions Dr. Thomas Smith 58
Moebes, Mike
   Cross-examines Tim Dunlap 68
Moore, Howard 85
Morgan County Courthouse 19, 21, 25
Morgan County Press 1

N

NAACP 8, 9, 41, 64, 85
Nettles, John 11, 12, 13, 26, 30, 41, 76, 77, 84, 96
   Over 1500 Hines' supporters march 101
Newcomb Street Church 4, 9, 11, 14, 15, 23, 41, 53
Newton, Demetrius 110
Nixon, Ray 15
North Central Alabama School for Developmentally Disabled 8
Notre Dame University 101

O

Old Town Community 2, 97, 100
Owens, Greg 69

P

Partlow 113, 114
   Deinstitutionalize 115
Pennylane Church of Christ 42
Peoples, Clem xii, 81, 87, 88, 91, 93
Peterson, Latrisha R. 98
Point Mallard 15
Post Office 18
Priest
   Russell 117
Purina Warehouse 92

R

Reeves, Steven 53
Revolutionary Communist Party 101
Rice, John Anthony xii, 22, 44, 82, 95
Rice, John Anthony
   Arrest during mayhem of counter-demonstrators 95
Riley, Jack 45, 47, 49, 54, 57, 60, 61, 63, 65, 71, 73, 86, 89, 90
   Ordered case to Jefferson County for second time 109
Robinson, Alfonzo xii, 4, 9, 11, 12, 13, 30, 53, 54, 97
Robinson, Curtis 18, 97, 109
   Guilty verdict 109
   Testify on his behalf 109
Royal, James xiv, 7
Russell, Keith 2, 3, 18, 52, 60, 61, 62

S

Scapegoat ix, 117, 118
SCLC 8, 9, 10, 11, 12, 13, 15, 20, 25, 26, 29, 30, 31, 44, 46, 47, 76, 78, 80, 84, 85, 88, 89, 91, 95, 101, 107, 114
   Morgan County Chapter organized 14
SCLC, mule caravan to Point Mallard 16
Scottsboro Boys xiv, 7
Seger, Edwin 70, 71, 72, 73
Self, Pack 16, 20, 92
Shuttlesworth, Fred 41
   Over 1500 Hines' supporters march 101
Sixth Amendment to the Constitution 90
Slate, Rudolph 15, 18
Smith, Larry 94
Smith, Nelson 30
Smith, Thomas 58, 59, 70, 71

Southern Poverty Law Center 108, 114
Southern Railway 17
Steele, Ray 92, 96
Stover, Tom xiv

T

Tent city 31
Thompson, James 110
Tip Top Foods 97
Turner, Arthur 87

V

Vivian, C. T.
    Over 1500 Hines' supporters march 101

W

Ward, Doyle 6, 8, 19, 30, 52, 61, 62, 63, 64, 68, 69
Ward, Van 30
Washington DC's Black Caucus 104
Wayman Chapel 91, 98, 101, 105
Westgate Shopping Center 15, 88
White, Danny xii, 23, 24, 30, 43, 80, 88, 89
White, Will, Sr. 15
Whitfield, Manuel 86, 87, 88
    Federal Court hearing 88
    Kidnapped and beaten 87
Wilkinson, Bill 32, 96, 104, 105
Williams, Ronald 88
Woods, Abraham 107
Woods, Barbara 1, 3
Wright, Rosemary 69
Wynn, Steve xii, 6, 9

About the Author

Peggy Allen Towns is a local historian of African American history. A native of Decatur, Alabama, her passion is preserving the voices and legacy of African Americans in her home town. She lectures and facilitates workshops on genealogy, local people and historical places. She is dedicated to identifying historic places, and as a result of her efforts, several sites have been listed on the Alabama Register of Landmarks and Heritage and the National Register of Historic Places. She has done extensive research documenting her family's history, which led to the discovery of a relative who served with the 110th United States Colored Infantry and the writing of her first book, *Duty Driven: The Plight of North Alabama's African Americans During the Civil War*. Her second book *Scottsboro Unmasked:Decatur's Story* is based on the Scottsboro Boys trials. It is the first of its genre to tell how this two landmark Supreme Court ruling case affected locals in Decatur, the site for all trials but the first.

Author Photo: C. Wally Terry